LIQUEURS
AND
SPIRITS

First published 1985 by
Octopus Books Limited
59 Grosvenor Street
London W1

© 1985 text: The Condé Nast Publications Limited
© 1985 illustrations: Octopus Books Limited

ISBN 0 7064 2530 8

Produced by Mandarin Publishers Limited
22a Westlands Road
Quarry Bay, Hong Kong

Printed in Spain

VOGUE

LIQUEURS AND SPIRITS

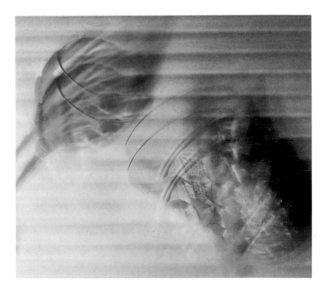

HENRY McNULTY
PHOTOGRAPHS BY TIM SIMMONS

OCTOPUS BOOKS

INTRODUCTION

Spirits, which cover all alcoholic beverages made by distillation rather than fermentation, can be sweetened and flavoured by maceration, percolation or distillation, to make literally hundreds of kinds of liqueurs. They derive their flavours from flowers and fruit, from herbs and spices, even from vegetables, and vary from the very sweet to the puckeringly dry. They can be drunk alone, mixed in cocktails, or as after-dinner digestifs, and, of course, many are used in cooking. Most of the old-time favourites, which include Bénédictine, Cointreau and Tia Maria, are in the high-strength bracket but there is a recent trend towards cream liqueurs and low-alcohol liqueurs.

Historically, there have been a number of different ways of expressing the strength of alcohol. In Britain, it used to be described in degrees proof (originally calculated by igniting gunpowder!), while in other countries it was calculated as its percentage of alcohol either in weight or by volume. Now, worldwide, strength is usually expressed as a percentage of alcohol by volume and this is the method adopted throughout this book. As a guide, the table below gives certain comparative strengths as they were formerly expressed in British proof, American proof and alcohol by volume (Gay-Lussac).

	BRITISH	AMERICAN	GAY–LUSSAC
Pure alcohol	75° over proof or 175° proof	200° proof	100%
	proof	114·2° proof	57·1%
	30° under proof or 70° proof	80° proof	40%
	65° under proof or 35° proof	40° proof	20%

A

AALBORG
The name of the firm which makes the best-known brand of the Danish spirit akvavit. It produces two types, one flavoured with caraway, the other mainly with dill. Founded in 1846, the Aalborg firm is probably the most famous in Denmark, and exports to over 100 countries. Recommended to accompany smoked salmon and creamed mushrooms. (See also *aquavit* and *schnapps*.)

ABRICOTINE
The brand name of an apricot liqueur made in France, at Enghien les Bains, near Paris, from apricots and their kernels, which are macerated with grape brandy.

ABSINTHE
The French word for the herb wormwood (from the Latin absinthium) and by extension for its essence, or a distillation of wine and other herbs, and wormwood. The clear extract turns a milky greeny-yellow when water is added to it. Known as the 'Green Goddess' in the last century, it acquired a bad reputation as the cause of many aberrations from sterility to insanity. As a result, absinthe has been

Absinthe

prohibited in most countries today. The concoction was drunk by dripping it through a perforated spoon that contained a lump or two of sugar. It had a high alcohol content and a strong taste of anis or liquorice.

Modern imitations which leave out the dangerous wormwood are popular in France and around the eastern Mediterranean, where they are known variously as pastis, ouzo or arak. In France two versions are made: Pernod tastes of anis, Ricard of liquorice. Both are now owned by Pernod, which, in a complete reversal of mores, now makes non-alcoholic pastis, known as Pacific, or Blancard.

ADVOCAAT

A very sustaining drink composed of grape brandy and egg yolks, beloved of nice old ladies, and chiefly popular in the Netherlands. It can also be made with a wine base. Most advocaat is low in alcohol (about 17%), and may have other flavours added, such as orange, lemon, vanilla or kirsch. It is also drunk combined with coffee, chocolate, lemonade or, more powerfully, cherry brandy. The biggest producers are the Dutch firms Bols, De Kuyper and Warninks.

SNOWBALL. Put 2 tablespoons of advocaat into a tall glass and top up with fizzy lemonade.

AGUARDIENTE

A Spanish word meaning 'burning water', which in Spain and Spanish-speaking America denotes an alcoholic distillation of grapes or molasses that provides a cheap substitute for brandy, whisky, or any other fire-water. The flavour varies but the effect is always the same.

ALEMBIC

A still — originally an Arab word, al ambique, meaning the same thing. The first record of one in Europe was said to be at Salerno in about A.D.1100. The Sicilians got the idea from the Arabs and used its output at the first known European medical school there. From its medical beginnings the uses of the still were soon developed into making a drinking spirit, which was flavoured with raisins to make a kind of primitive liqueur. This secret arrived in France a couple of centuries later. Before long, the 'schnapps devil' had almost taken control in Middle Europe. Monasteries all over Europe began making spirits as medicine at first, then flavouring them so they became palatable as well as being medicinal.

AMANDES, Crème d'

Sweet liqueur made from a macedoine of almonds and steeped in brandy.

AMARETTO

The almond flavour of this infused liqueur derives from apricot kernels and seeds. It is rich and sweet, marvellous as a sauce for vanilla icecream, and excellent taken straight. It is supposed to have been invented by a beautiful female innkeeper who posed for the Italian painter Bernardino Luini as the Madonna in his fresco of the nativity at Saronno. She thanked him for that, and perhaps other favours, with her recipe. The best-known brand is Amaretto di Saronno.

CAFFÉ PUCCI. Mix 1 fl oz each amaretto and rum, pour into a large cup of coffee and add whipped cream.
SMOOTH SICILIAN. One part Southern Comfort, one part Amaretto di Saronno, shaken with ice.

AMER PICON

A pungent bitters invented in the 1830s by an officer of the French army in Algiers, Gaston Picon. Presumably he thought it would be good for malaria, for it contains quinine as well as gentian and orange. Very popular in France with ice and soda, or with gin.

AMERICAN WHISKEY

Immigrants from the 'Old Country' brought the art of distillation with them to the New World. At first, however, they found barley too difficult to grow, so they began to use a mash (grain combined with water) of the grains that did thrive in the harsh pioneer days – maize (corn) and rye.

That they were successful almost at once is shown by the fact that whiskey (spelt with an 'e') was already so popular by 1791 that an attempt by the infant republic to tax it two years later was met by the new union's first important rebellion, 'The Whiskey Rebellion'. Producers who could do so moved their stills off to the 'Wild West', to Kentucky and western Pennsylvania; some even went to Canada. There or thereabouts they have stayed, though American whiskey can be made anywhere in the U.S.A. where it conforms to regulations.

The majority of whiskey production in the U.S.A. is made from 60 to 70% corn and is called bourbon, because it was in Kentucky's Bourbon County that most of the producers set up shop.

Famous bourbon names include Jim Beam, Taylor, Old Crow, Old Grandad and Old Forrester. Equal in fame is Jack Daniels, which is not a bourbon, but is made in Tennessee. Next comes rye, made mostly in Pennsylvania and Maryland. There is also a lower quality simply called corn whiskey.

It is important to look for the word 'straight' on an American whiskey label, because it indicates that the spirit is of one type only, and has been aged at least two years in oak. Blended American whiskey must contain at least one part in five of American straight whiskey. The term 'Bottled in bond' tells you it has been stored in a government bonded warehouse for four years, but is not a guarantee of quality.

ANANAS, Crème d'

Rather an exotic liqueur, made from pineapples and strongly flavoured. Often rum-based, since pineapples and sugarcane seem to grow in similar climates, it is usually aged well in wood. There are Hawaiian versions, and a Dutch one.

ANGOSTURA

Perhaps the world's most famous and ubiquitous bitters, this 'medicine' is another cure-all invented by a soldier (see **amer picon**). Dr. J. G. B. Siegert, a German veteran of the Napoleonic wars, went off to help Simón Bolívar liberate Bolivia. While inventing his bitters, he also succeeded in bringing up nine offspring in a Venezuelan town at first named after his hero, Ciudad Bolivar, but later renamed Angostura. Dr. Siegert named the bitters after the town in which he lived.

One of his brood decided to move away from Venezuelan authority. He set up in Trinidad, where, as an old Calypso stated, 'all the people were glad', in Port of Spain. The firm remains there to this day. **A**lfonso XIII of Spain appointed Angostura supplier to his court in 1907, as did other monarchs, including George VI of England, George V of Sweden, and now Queen Elizabeth II. Their patronage has helped the bitters to fame, and the family to fortune. **B**ecause of their German nationality, in World War II the family lost their ownership of the brand, but the fourth-generation heir, Robert Siegert, managed to get back into the company. Together with his father, he finally regained control. Now the fifth generation is in charge.

Angostura is used in almost every bar in the world, private or public, for mixing drinks, and by many a chef in cooking. Like most liqueurs and bitters, its contents are secret, but its label proclaims it 'skilfully blended with gentian, combined with harmless vegetable spices'. (See also **bitters**.)

PINK LIME. This is a refreshing variation of the well-known pink gin, made famous through its popularity with the British Navy. Fill a cocktail glass with crushed ice, put in 4 drops of Angostura bitters and a teaspoonful of lime juice, top up with gin and add a twist of lemon or lime.

*A*NIS

The generic name for a liqueur obtained from an infusion of aniseed berries diluted in a neutral spirit. (Star anise is not used.) Although aniseed is a member of the hemlock family, it is fortunately not a deadly poison. Its flavour, something like liquorice, is a favourite all around the Mediterranean. Since the Dark Ages anis has been almost universally used as a cure for stomach ailments. In Spain, it is a popular aperitif. Anis del Mono and Anis de Chinchón are two well-known brands. Spanish anis is either sweet or dry, and is usually drunk diluted with water. The French, too, like anis, but as a liqueur, Anisette, which is sweet, alcoholic and strong.

*A*NISETTE

Originally used as a tonic and aphrodisiac in eighteenth-century France, this liqueur is a sweet infusion of aniseed in spirits. There are several brands. The one produced by Marie Brizard in about 1750 is still being made. Mme Brizard obtained the recipe from a West African whom she had befriended, and first used it as a medicine. The addition of sugar transformed the medicine into a popular liqueur. The patronage of the Duc de Richelieu guaranteed the success of Mme Brizard and her discovery.

*A*PPLEJACK

American apple brandy. George Washington inquired about a recipe for it in about 1760. Abraham Lincoln is on record as having sold apple brandy for 12 cents a half-pint in his native city, Springfield, before he became a politician. Americans now tend to use it as an after-dinner liqueur, or in cooking, as the French do with Calvados (q.v.).

*A*PRICOT BRANDY

A distillation or maceration of apricot kernels with

their partly fermented fruit, in grain or wine alcohol. In western Europe it is often sweet, but in eastern Europe and the Middle East it can be fiercely dry and strong. It is made in Yugoslavia, Bulgaria and Rumania, but the Hungarian version, Barak Pálinka, is the best.

AQUAVIT

Used in Scandinavia, along with akvavit and akavit, to denote a grain spirit in which various herbs are infused to give flavour. It is, in effect, a flavoured vodka. In Denmark the flavour usually comes from caraway and dill. In Norway aquavit is unflavoured but aged. The Swedes drink it sweet or dry, flavouring it with fennel, aniseed, caraway and even bitter orange. The Germans like cumin as a flavour. Confusingly, aquavit is also often known as schnapps (in Germany) or snaps (in Sweden and Norway).

You are supposed to drink aquavit very cold – like vodka – in tiny glasses, and down each glass in one gulp, but I prefer to sip it – especially the Norwegian version – to savour its aged voluptuousness. There is much Scandinavian hocus-pocus about looking your neighbour in the eye as the aquavit goes down, but that custom is de rigueur only in its homeland! Before he was President, Ronald Reagan became a member of an aquavit club, the Guild of Christian IV (King of Denmark), the initiation ceremony of which includes having to sing 'Down with juice and tea, snaps is the drink for me'. (See also **bommerlunder** and **schnapps**.)

DANISH MARY. *This is made like its cousin, Bloody Mary, with tomato juice and Worcestershire sauce, but with aquavit instead of vodka.*

ARGENTARIUM

A delicious infusion of herbs, this liqueur is made by Passionist Fathers in a huge, almost empty monastery 60 miles north of Rome and is very popular locally. It is one of the few liqueurs the manufacture and sale of

*which is still managed directly by monks, who roam
the nearby hills in search of 13 necessary herbs (as
well as using some commercial sources of supply).*

ARMAGNAC

*Armagnac should take out patents as a perfume. Its
supporters claim that, when young, it has the scent of
violets. As it matures, it takes on the aroma of prunes
(not mere ordinary prunes, but those of Agen, when
they are being removed from the drying oven). It is also
accused of smelling like lime-tree blossoms, fresh
vanilla beans, green hazelnuts, over-ripe quinces,
yellow peaches, and freshly crushed peppercorns.*

Armagnac is made of white wine from one of three
areas — Bas-Armagnac, Ténarèze, or Haut-Armagnac
— and may have one of those names on the label,
unless it is a mixture of two or more, when it can only
claim to be 'armagnac'. It is distilled in continuous stills,
not 'batch' stills. The new spirit is aged in barrels of
local 'black' oak, which passes on its dark hue to the
brandy (in Cognac, of course, barrels of Limousin oak
are used). Ageing takes from a minimum of one year
to 15 or 20 years. Its age, as indicated on the label, is
that of the youngest brandy in the bottle. Adding a
20-year-old armagnac to a five-year-old one does not
'average out' to a twelve-and-a-half-year-old drink!
Look for the words 'Bas-Armagnac' on the label. That
is the section of the producing area that makes the
best quality brandy, and produces about half the total
output. If you insist on the absolute best, you should
ask for 'Grand-Bas-Armagnac', or 'Grand Bas'.

Armagnac is still a relatively small village industry.
Among the best known brands are: Janneau,
Samalens, Lafontan, Marquis de Montesquieu, Mar-
quis de Puységur, and Sempé.

> **ARMAGNAC COCKTAILS. One part brandy to two parts
> orange juice (plus sugar, soda water and ice, if you like)
> makes a pleasant drink. One part each armagnac and lemon
> juice with two parts champagne or sparkling wine is a
> version of the 'French 75'. One-third each armagnac,
> triple-sec and lemon juice with lots of ice is refreshing.**

ARRACK (Araki, Raki, Rakija)

East Indian arrack, popular in Sumatra, Borneo, Java, New Guinea and other exotic parts, is usually made from a base of sugarcane, coconut liquor or rice wine and other local sources of ferment. When made from molasses it tastes much like rum. Javan Batavia Arrack is perhaps the best type.

East Indian arrack should not be confused with the quite different drink of the same name found around the Balkans and Mediterranean. Palm wine was distilled into arrack in Palmyra, in the Arab Mediterranean, as long ago as 800 B.C. Because of the Moslem ban on alcohol, very little arrack is made legally today. It is still available as a rather powerful white alcohol of uncertain quality, produced from grapes or raisins, or, in North Africa, from figs. Tunisia's Boukha fig liqueur is very drinkable. Greek raki is a fairly raw white fire-water, and similar potent alcohols are to be found in Bulgaria and Yugoslavia under different names. Yugoslav rakija is made from plum spirits.

ATHOLL BROSE

A Scottish concoction (well, almost a porridge) that has been bottled and turned into a kind of liqueur. It is made of malt whisky, honey, cream and oatmeal plus the usual secret ingredients. It has a most particular flavour, and it may be an advantage to be a Scot to appreciate it.

AURUM (potabile)

A golden triple-sec from Italy's Abruzzi mountains. Coloured with saffron, flavoured with oranges, orange zests and herbs, steeped in brandy. French master chef Raymond Oliver suggests that aurum potabile is 'the most ancient of all liqueurs' and further surmises that it was a forerunner of Goldwasser (q.v.) with 'real' gold flecks floating in it.

B

B AND B

A mixture of approximately half brandy and half Bénédictine. The idea began in the 1930s, just after Prohibition ended in the U.S.A. Liqueur fanciers found Bénédictine alone too sweet, and mixed it with brandy at home. The result was a drink so popular that it is now being bottled, already mixed, by the venerable Bénédictine distillery itself.

BANANES, Crème de

A very sweet liqueur made of ripe bananas that have been macerated in pure neutral spirits. It has an appropriately yellow tinge, and a strong banana taste and aroma. It is mainly used as a flavouring agent in cocktails such as Banana Daiquiri (a mixture of rum, crème de bananes, lime juice, sugar and crushed ice). Because of its rather heavy texture, with both crème de bananes and the drier version, Banadry, a little goes a long way.

BARAK PÁLINKA

A dry Hungarian apricot brandy, made near the city of Kecskemét. The same area produces a sweet apricot liqueur, called Kecskeméti Barak. Some Barak Pálinka is also made in Austria by the Zwack family.

BÉNÉDICTINE

One of several medicinal liqueurs first concocted by a monastic order in about 1510 at Fécamp, in Normandy, and now a purely secular business. Like Chartreuse, Bénédictine was banned after the French Revolution. The abbey of Fécamp was closed and the recipe – naturally a well-kept secret – was lost, until Alexandre LeGrand, a descendant of the family that had handled the abbey's legal affairs, found it among some old documents. In about 1863, he began to make an up-dated version. Today, with double-distilled brandy and some 75 different herbs and spices among the ingredients, its flavour has been described as 'flamboyant Gothic', an epithet equally befitting its fantastic distillery, built by old Alexandre.

The initials D.O.M. on Bénédictine bottles are short for what its monkish inventor is reputed to have exclaimed on first tasting his brew – 'Deo optimo maximo!' (Praise to God most good, most great!)

DRY MONASTIC. This is two parts Bénédictine, three parts Cinzano red and one part gin.
WHISKY SCAFFA. Mix half Bénédictine and half whisky, plus a dash of Angostura.

BITTERS

Mind-boggling, stomach-settling, medicinal affairs, bitters are concentrations of herbs, spices, roots or bark, steeped in, or distilled with, spirits. Originally bitters were concocted by apothecaries to be used as cures for sickness, or as elixirs. They can be compounded by anyone, almost anywhere, but the most famous one – Angostura (q.v.) – comes from Trinidad. France, Italy, Germany and the Netherlands all produce and consume dozens of different brands. The U.S.A. and U.K. also produce a fair number, as do Spain and Portugal. French names include Amer Picon, Quinquina, St Raphaël and Byrrh. Italy's are legion, including Punt e Mes, Fernet Branca, Campari, China Martini, Amaro Montenegro and Radis. Every Italian bar displays at least half a dozen different local brands. An Austro-Hungarian one, also made in Italy,

is Unicum. Germany offers Underberg. In the U.S.A. are Abbots and Peychaud. Holland makes a Boone-kamp and Welling.

Bitters may be used either as a flavouring in mixed drinks, or as aperitifs. In Italy, especially, they are commonly used in both ways. The flavour types include innumerable orange, apricot and peach bitters which can be added to mixed drinks and often to food recipes. Fernet Branca makes Branca-menta, a drinking bitters that also combines well with ice and soda to form an agreeable, non-sweet aperitif.

Buy bitters in miniature bottles so that you can experiment with different kinds.

BLACKBERRY BRANDY
See *eau-de-vie*.

BLACKBERRY LIQUEUR
See *fruit liqueur* and *mûres, crème de*.

BLACKCURRANT LIQUEUR
See *cassis*.

BOLS
The trade name of an important Dutch producer of various liqueurs and spirits, but perhaps best known for a spirit, Dutch gin or genever (q.v.). The firm makes over a dozen other liqueurs and spirits, including Blue (and other hues) Curaçao, crème de bananes, crème de menthe, and apricot brandy.

BOMMERLUNDER
A top-selling German aquavit made in Flensburg, on the Danish border, since the eighteenth century. This was another miraculous discovery from an 'un-known's' pocket. The story is that a wounded warrior,

while fleeing from one of Frederick the Great's defeats, arrived at a Flensburg inn penniless, and offered the innkeeper his treasured, yellowed document with its unusual aquavit recipe as payment. The recipe made such good drinking that eventually King Frederick of Denmark appointed its new owner as Royal aquavit supplier. It tastes dry and 'wholesome'.

*B*OURBON WHISKEY

The most popular kind of American whiskey. Corn (maize) is the principal ingredient used. The law dictates that the mash from which it is distilled must contain at least 51% corn, and the distillation cannot be stronger than 100° U.S. proof, 50% alcohol. It is aged for at least two years in charred white oak barrels. 'Bottled in bond' bourbon has been aged for a minimum of four years in government-supervised warehouses. This is no guarantee of quality, however, apart from its greater age. 'Sour Mash' bourbon is made from a mash that has yeast in it, left over from previous fermentations.

*B*RANDY

Strictly speaking, brandy is a spirit distilled only from grape wines, but today the word is also used to include fruit distillations like plum, apple, and berry brandies (q.v.).

Almost universally considered to set the criteria for excellence in true brandies are the French armagnac and cognac. Huge quantities of grape brandy are also made in Italy, Spain, Portugal, Greece, Germany, the U.S.A., Australia, South Africa and other countries. There is a delicious variety made in Chile and Peru called Pisco, which bears the characteristic aroma of the muscat grapes from which it is distilled. But none compares with the two leaders.

What distinguishes all these brandy delights one from another is the tiny quantity of aldehydes, acid salts, and other imperfections hidden among them. Were it *not for these 'impurities', whisky, brandy, rum and vodka would all taste pretty much alike. The best brandy is made mainly in pot stills and aged for long periods in wood.*

The word brandy is a corruption of the Dutch brande wijn *and, as seems to happen when terms are transferred from one language to another (as with the French* un dry *for a dry martini, or* le self *for a self-service restaurant), the English version retains only the first and perhaps least important of the two words –* brande *simply means 'burnt'.*

Calvados (q.v.) is an apple brandy from Normandy. Spanish and Portuguese brandies taste sweeter than the French, with more flavour of the wood in which they are stored. They are 'comfortable' drinks with a pleasant bouquet.

Cyprus, South Africa and Australia also make brandies that have their own characters and flavours. California is another producer. American brandy is clean and light. Christian Brothers, Paul Masson, Korbel and Cresta Blanca are some of the good names. German Brantwein is made from grapes. Asbach Uralt is as similar to cognac as any 'foreign' brand can be. Italy has a sweetish, grapey brandy called Stock and claims to produce 50 million bottles of the spirit annually.

The more traditional white framboise and its cousins, poire Williams (from pears), kirsch (from cherries) and mirabelle (from small, absolutely delicious yellow plums), are all dry brandies, and make joyous drinking cold, or sprinkled over fresh cream.

Part of the enjoyment of any brandy is its aroma. It is often served in balloon glasses, but I prefer it in ordinary tulip-shaped wine glasses. The balloon concentrates the fumes to such an extent that they are almost overpowering, while the tulip allows the brandy to release its flavour and fragrance without suffocating the drinker.

BRANDY SMASH. Crush a few sprigs of mint with a teaspoon of sugar and place in a glass. Add a splash of soda water, 2 ice cubes and 1½ fl oz brandy.

ARCO-IRIS (meaning 'rainbow') is a Portuguese idea which is equal parts of crème de cacao, crème de violettes, yellow

Chartreuse, maraschino, green Chartreuse or Izzara, and brandy. Each should float on the other layers, so pour carefully and slowly.

BRANDY SLING. This requires 2 fl oz brandy or cognac, the juice of 1 lemon, sugar to taste and a dash of Angostura bitters. Pour into a tall glass filled with ice and plain water, and stir.

BRANDY SCAFFA (if you are in a sweetish mood) is served unchilled and undiluted. It is made with that same dash of Angostura, then equal parts of maraschino and brandy.

BRIZARD, MARIE

One of the best-known names in French liqueur production. Marie Brizard, born in 1714, was lucky enough to inherit the 'secret' recipe for anisette, which she and her nephew began to manufacture with huge success. A 17-herb concoction, distilled with anis in alcohol, it is still the biggest seller of its kind in France, and is one of 30 or so liqueurs in the family-owned Bordeaux firm's line.

BROMBEERGEIST

A popular German liqueur based on a maceration of wild blackberries.

BYRRH

If you go into a French café and ask for a beer, it is likely that Byrrh is what will be set in front of you, for the word is pronounced just like the familiar malt-hops-yeast-water beverage you find in your favourite pub. (French for beer is pronounced 'bee-air'.) Byrrh, however, is a bitters, made with quinine and wine, with a brandy booster. It is very popular in France. (See also **quinquina**.)

CACAO, Crème de

Cacao is the plant from the seeds of which both cocoa and chocolate are produced. Crème de cacao is a sweetened distillation of the cacao beans combined with, and infused or percolated with, vanilla to produce a chocolate-flavoured liqueur. It is often combined with other flavours, among them cherries, coconut, mint (Royal Mint-Chocolate is one of the latest in these lines) or oranges (Sabra, from Israel). Other kinds of chocolate liqueur include: Chéri Suisse from Switzerland, Vandermint from Holland, and Marie Brizard Cacao from France.

CAFÉ, Crème de

Like crème de cacao, this is an almost universally liked type of liqueur, made from an infusion of coffee with a spirit, usually rum. Tia Maria is from Jamaica and made with that island's fabulous Blue Mountain coffee and local rum. Kahlúa is made with Mexican coffee, and its home is Mexico City. The basis of Irish Velvet is Irish whiskey. Zwack Viennese Café is coffee with neutral spirits. Marie Brizard Café from France is slightly liquorice-flavoured.

A novel, if messy, way to take liqueurs was practised a hundred years or so ago by the Earl of Effingham and his lady, who would sit opposite each other at dinner at the Duke of Mecklenburg-Strelitz's court. He would feed her liqueur chocolates by throwing them across the table into her mouth, to the vast amusement of the Duke and his friends.

CALISAY

A herbal liqueur from Catalonia, made from barks, such as chinchona, which gives us quinine, and aged in oak. As one might expect, its mystery recipe came from a monastery – this time located in Bohemia.

CALVADOS

Brandy made from apples in Normandy. Calvados is a remarkably aristocratic spirit, with a beautiful nose, the equal of fine cognac or armagnac when it is ten or more years old. Cider is the basis from which this spirit is distilled. It is a cottage industry, in which most distilling is done on private farms, in pot stills. It can be amusing to tour the Pays d'Auge, the principal production area, and drop in for tastings at the source. A 'fire-water' is also made from apple peel left over from cider making, called eau-de-vie de marc de cidre – a drink to be wary of!

When young, calvados can taste like swallowing a nutmeg grater, but a properly aged one, fifteen years old, say, is an after-dinner delight. In the U.S.A. this kind of brandy is called Applejack, of which Laird's is perhaps the best known. (As schoolboys we used to make our own by letting cider freeze, with a straw inserted into the centre of the frozen block. The alcohol remained liquid and could be poured off through the straw to drink as apple brandy.)

CAMPARI

A 'drinking bitters', aggressively red in colour, not quite as violently bitter as some, and very drinkable with soda water. It is blended with multi-national 'secret' herbs, mellowed in spirits and matured in oak

vats. A Campari-Soda, however, is a ready-mixed and
bottled version. I prefer to mix my own, with soda
water and a slice of lemon.

AMERICANO. This is a Campari drink made with ½
Campari and ½ red vermouth, with a slice of lemon and ice.
ORA SHAKEROTO. Mix Campari with an egg white, then
shake with ice till it hurts.

CANADIAN WHISKY

Blended whisky from grain, mostly corn (maize) and
rye. It is inclined to be made in continuous stills that
resemble petrol cracking plants. It must, by law, be
matured for three years. Four big firms dominate the
Canadian whisky market. The biggest is Seagrams, the
world's most extensive liqueur producer; the others
are Hiram Walker, Gilbey Canada and Canadian
Schenley.

CARAWAY

A herb used in gin, and in many liqueurs (see
kümmel).

CASCARILLA

South American speciality of barks, spices and brandy.

CASSIS

Properly known as crème de cassis, this is an extract of
blackcurrants, with about 15% of alcohol by volume.
Rich in vitamin C, the currant juice is infused with sugar
for a couple of months in a sort of molasses-rum
mixture. Cassis is used for mixing, and nowadays is
especially popular with white wine as an aperitif, in the
form of a Kir. (About 10 parts of wine to one of cassis
is my Kir formula, to avoid too much sweetness.) It can
also be used to flavour vermouth or champagne, or
any other wine or spirit – invent your own recipe.

Crème de cassis is sold by Bouchard Aîné, Marie
Brizard, Giffard, Cartron and many others in France.

CHARTREUSE

One of the few liqueurs first made in a monastery and still controlled by monks. It was invented in 1605 by monks of the Carthusian order, and takes its name from La Grande Chartreuse, 'the great charterhouse' near Grenoble in France, which is the mother house. Within this forbidding edifice, resembling a small fortified town, a vow of silence is observed.

At the time of the French Revolution, the Carthusians were evicted, and banned from making their elixir. Some moved to Tarragona in Spain, taking their formula with them, and continued to make Chartreuse. It was not until 1931 that the French government finally allowed the Order to resume making Chartreuse in Grenoble.

Green Chartreuse is one of the strongest liqueurs at 55% alcohol. Yellow Chartreuse is weaker at 43%. The base is brandy enhanced with various herbs, their identity a secret as usual, and supposedly known only to three monks. The recipe is thought to include balm, hyssop, angelica, cinnamon, saffron and mace among the 135 kinds used. Whatever the formula, its flavour and aroma are delicious. It can be taken straight or on the rocks, and is an excellent flavouring for icecream and other dishes. Green Chartreuse is comparatively dry tasting and powerful. Yellow is almost like a flavoured honey.

The manufacture of the liqueur is no longer handled in La Grande Chartreuse itself, but some 15 miles away at Voiron. The drink became so popular that the Order, which abhors publicity, moved the distillery out to get some peace. All profits from the sale of the Chartreuse go to the Order, which, after deducting its operating expenses, distributes them to charities, and to other religious causes. Even the advertising and promotion expenses of the liqueur are borne by the Chartreuse agents around the world. The monks have of course kept themselves completely isolated from the commercial aspects of the business.

CUPID'S BOW. Use 1 fl oz each of Chartreuse and gin and lemon juice, with a dash of Grenadine.

CHERRY BRANDY

This name is generally used to describe sweet liqueurs made by infusing cherry juice with spirits. These are not, therefore, true brandies. This makes for a very confusing appellation, as most cherry 'brandies' are really cherry liqueurs. True cherry brandy is what the French call 'white alcohol', like their kirsch and other fruit brandies. German kirsch, too, is distilled directly from the fermented juice of cherries and is, therefore, a true cherry brandy.

Nevertheless, cherry brandy, the liqueur, is widely admired and consumed throughout Europe. Among the best-known brands are Cherry Rocher, Peter Heering, Dolfi, De Kuyper, Garnier, not to mention Scandinavian, German and Swiss brands.

CHERRY HEERING

So well known was Cherry Heering as a cherry brandy that it rates a line or two of its own. The family is now trying to establish a new, more accurate, description for it as 'Peter Heering Cherry Liqueur', after its Danish inventor of 150 years ago. It is made from dark native Zeeland cherries, and aged in huge antique oak casks. Whether other brands of 'cherry brandy' will follow suit on nomenclature is questionable.

CHINA

Pronounced 'kina', this is the Italian name for the Spanish chinchona, or the French quinquina liqueurs. All are varieties of a popular bitter type of aperitif-liqueur flavoured with the bark of the chinchona tree, from which we get quinine. Italians are particularly fond of quinine as an ingredient for bitters.

These liqueurs were first used as medicines to treat malaria. The bark was named by the naturalist Linnaeus in honour of a former representative of the Queen of Spain in Peru. This lady, the Countess of Chinchon, suffered from malaria and found that the bark greatly relieved the symptoms of the disease. She *introduced chinchona to Europe in about 1740. For about 300 years afterwards it was the only remedy for malaria, until World War II, when a more effective cure was discovered.*

CHINCHONA
See china.

CHINESE WINE
A misnomer, since most Chinese (and Japanese) wine is actually a low-potency spirit which can be made from all sorts of ingredients, ranging from grapes to bamboo shoots as well as rice. Mao-Tai is perhaps the best known Chinese spirit in Europe, partly because it was used for toasts on President Nixon's friendship trip to Peking in 1972. It is only some 25% alcohol, but other types can reach as much as 51%. Chinese spirits are an acquired taste, to say the least. And that goes for Japanese too, in my book.

CHOCOLATE
See cacao.

COCONUT LIQUEURS
In recent times, there has been a sudden spate of coconut-flavoured alcohols. Among them are Coco-ribe Liqueur, Malibu, made with a white rum base, Batida de Coco, a Brazilian drink with coconut-flavoured alcohol of 16% alcohol by volume, and others. French and Dutch producers also make coconut liqueurs. Most coconut liqueurs are used for mixing cocktails.

**COCONUT COCKTAILS. Blend 3 fl oz Malibu with the juice of 1 lemon, 1 fl oz pineapple juice, and 1 fl oz cream.
OR 2 fl oz Cocoribe with 2 fl oz tea, and sugar to taste. Pour over ice and add a squeeze of lemon juice.
OR Batida de Coco mixed with orange juice or crème de menthe in proportions suited to your own taste.**

30

COFFEE LIQUEURS

Almost as soon as it was imported into Europe from the Americas in the early eighteenth century, coffee began to be made into liqueurs. Countries that like their coffee strong seem to have a corresponding fondness for coffee liqueur. Italy has an Espresso, a Gala Caffé and a Caboco; Brazil has Bahia; Jamaica has Tia Maria; Mexico has Kahlúa; the French have Kamok (a name derived from café-mocha); Turkey has Pasha, and even Ireland has Irish Velvet, for instant Irish coffees when you add hot water.

COGNAC

Only brandy from the Charente region of France is legitimately cognac. This area lies in the west, not far from La Rochelle. The wine from the Charente vineyards is so acid it is practically undrinkable as wine, but it distils superbly, a process handled mainly by the farmers themselves – some eight thousand of them. Because the small farmers do not have enough storage space, the spirit is then sent to the big shipping houses like Courvoisier, Hine, Martell, Hennessy, Rémy Martin, and Bisquit Dubouché, to name but a few, for blending and ageing.

The shippers age the spirit in oak kegs stored in huge warehouses. Brandy does not go on ageing forever, and some experts say it reaches its prime at about 40 years. Most of what we drink is between four and 12 years old. The wine is distilled in burnished, onion-shaped copper stills. Once distilling starts it must be kept up continuously, day and night, until the whole supply of wine has become brandy. This means that the workmen must sleep on the job to keep the boilers burning and the wine flowing into the stills.

Newly made cognac is colourless and is poured into huge vats to blend. It is then transferred into the kegs that are to hold it for the next four or five years or more as it matures. A good deal is lost from each keg through evaporation as the liquid seeps through the wood, but though the makers deplore this loss, it is a

31

necessary part of the process that turns fire-water into a smooth after-dinner drink.

Once bottled, brandy ceases to age, so don't be fooled by a cobwebby bottle into thinking it must be old. All those stars and letters on the labels likewise do not necessarily indicate age. V.S.O.P. simply means 'very superior old pale'. The rest of the lettering system is as easy to work out: F for fine, X for extra, C for cognac – what else, indeed?

Since cognacs are a blend, and since every famous producer tries to maintain the same character in his cognac each year, the way to decide which brand you prefer is to experiment until you find the taste you like best at the price you want to pay. The Rémy Martin version is dark and caramelly; Courvoisier is sharper, while Camus, Hine, Martell, Otard and Monnet are each distinguished in their own way. Because it should average ten to twelve years of age, V.S.O.P. is the best buy in terms of value for money.

Simply 2 fl oz cognac in orange juice with ice is excellent. STINGER: This is the famous cognac cocktail. Use one-half each cognac and white crème de menthe, shake with ice and strain into a glass.

*C*OINTREAU

This famed liqueur began life as Triple-sec, but before long was being so widely imitated that the name was changed to avoid suffering from the sincerest form of flattery. It is made with a combination of bitter West Indian orange peel, and oranges from the sunny Côte d'Azur for flavouring, plus the usual plethora of mysterious ingredients.

Founded over 100 years ago in Angers, France, where it still has its headquarters, the firm is the biggest manufacturer of liqueurs in France. It also produces Cointreau in both North and South America and in Spain. It has a rum distillery in Martinique, and shelters a host of other liqueurs and wines under its corporate umbrella.

Clear white Cointreau, in its square bottle, is, however, by far the firm's most successful product. The White

*Lady (see **gin**), and Cointreau-on-the-Rocks (the very
idea of which would have shocked its inventor) are
probably the most popular cocktails.*

> **CONCORDE.** Mix 1 fl oz each of Cointreau and dry
> vermouth, plus 2 fl oz vodka and pour over cracked ice.
> **SIDECAR.** Blend one-quarter cointreau, one-half brandy
> and one-quarter lemon juice, and shake with ice. (Invented in
> Paris by an army officer who kept going back and forth to the
> Café Dôme on his motorcycle sidecar.)

CORDIAL MÉDOC

*It will surprise no one to learn that this liqueur comes
from Bordeaux. A blend of orange, cherries, brandy,
curaçao, claret and herbs, it is reddish in colour, rather
like an old sherry, and has a light clean taste.*

CORDIALS

*Americans occasionally use this term to mean liqueurs.
The name is derived from the Latin cordialis, meaning
'of the heart', because such libations were supposed
to be useful as a heart stimulant. In the U.K., the word
usually refers to a non-alcoholic flavoured drink.*

CORN

*A whiskey made from a mash of corn (or maize) in the
U.S.A., where it is the main ingredient in America's
favourite spirit, bourbon whiskey (q.v.). 'Corn' is also
drunk as 'corn whiskey', having its own appellation.*

CRÈME

*A term originally used to imply excellence (crème de la
crème). A liqueur described on the label as 'crème'
indicates that it either has a taste which is exclusively
that of the flavouring named, or that it has such a
flavour predominating. Crème d'ananas, for instance,
is a pineapple liqueur, Crème de menthe is mint, and
so on. (See under specific flavour names.) It is,
however, also used to describe mixtures of spirits
(whisky, brandy, rum) with real cream.*

CRÈME DE MENTHE FRAPPÉE. Fill a small glass with crushed ice and pour the crème de menthe over – to the brim. Serve with a straw.

CUARANTA Y TRES

A popular Spanish liqueur containing herbs and sugar, made in Cartagena from an old Carthaginian recipe, they say. It has a vanilla flavour.

CUMIN

A herb used for flavouring liqueurs and a relative of the caraway. Denmark used to produce a good white cumin liqueur called Cuminum Liquidum Optimum Castelli, C.L.O.C. for short, meaning 'the best cumin liqueur in the castle'. (Unfortunately, C.L.O.C. seems to have disappeared. Perhaps the castle was razed?)

CURAÇAO

Strangely enough, the word curaçao is not a trade name but a generic one for a specific variety of orange liqueur. Originally this drink was known as triple-sec (q.v.), which was an anomaly, because a triple-sec is definitely not dry but very sweet. It is made in many countries by many companies. The Dutch popularized their version, flavoured with dried peel from the bitter oranges of their Caribbean colony, Curaçao.

APRÈS SKI. Mix 1½ fl oz apricot brandy and 1½ fl oz of curaçao with the juice of 1 lemon and add a twist of peel. Shake with ice.

BLANCHE. Blend 1 fl oz each curaçao, anisette and cointreau. Shake with ice.

RUBY PUNCH. Combine a bottle of sparkling burgundy with 2 fl oz each brandy, curaçao and raspberry syrup, the juice of a lemon and orange, and a bottle of soda water mixed in at the last moment.

Try a half grapefruit (or orange halves) sprinkled with brown sugar with a pat (1 oz) of butter on top and 1 teaspoon of curaçao on each half. Grill until sugar is melted.

CYNAR

An Italian liqueur made from artichoke hearts.

DANZIGER GOLDWASSER

Literally translated as 'gold water from Danzig' this is one of the best known of the liqueurs that contain tiny specks of gold. Flavoured with caraway and other herbs, they are popular in Germany and other Middle European and Scandinavian countries. During the Middle Ages, gold was thought to be beneficial for various illnesses and caraway good for the digestion, so this dry libation combines two 'medicinal' ingredients. Danziger Silberwasser is a similar beverage, but contains silver flakes.

DEMERARA RUM

A dark rum that originally came from Guyana. It is a strong, full-bodied, heavy, fruity type, often used for flavouring cake or making grog.

GROG. For this warming drink use 2 teaspoons brown Demerara rum, the juice of half a lemon, 2 cloves and a pinch of nutmeg. Fill the glass with boiling water and stir with a cinnamon stick.

DIGESTIF

A word used in Europe for an after-dinner drink, usually a liqueur, but often, too, a spirit, like cognac. In both Italy and Spain such drinks are called digestivos. As the word implies, liqueurs in general are supposed to help digestion, and, because of their herbal content, many of them probably do have a mildly beneficial effect when taken in moderation. In France, any liqueur or spirit is a digestif, but Larousse says 'They do not deserve the name'!

D ISTILLATION

A method of extracting alcohol from a fermented fruit juice or other liquid containing natural alcohol. This is done by heating the liquid to boiling point, whereupon the alcohol, being more volatile than water, rises in steam. The steam is condensed by cooling and becomes more or less pure alcohol. A first distillation may be redistilled to produce purer and purer – nearly 100% – alcohol. The result is usually diluted with water to reduce its total alcoholic strength to anything from 79% alcohol down to 17% before it is used in the making of a spirit or a liqueur.

D RAMBUIE

A peppery Scottish liqueur made from aged malt whisky, sweetened with heather honey and flavoured with herbs. The story goes that after escaping from his defeat at the Battle of Culloden in 1745 the refugee pretender to the throne of England, Prince Charles Edward Stuart of Scotland (Bonnie Prince Charlie), found a hideaway on the Isle of Skye. His protector was a Captain Mackinnon, who managed to whisk the Prince off to France and safety. The grateful Prince gave Mackinnon his family recipe for 'the drink that satisfies', or 'an dram buidheach'. Today, it ranks among the world's most sought-after liqueurs, still being made by descendants of the Mackinnons, the biggest liqueur producers in Britain.

D UBONNET

A type of vermouth (q.v.), and a proprietary name, but so well known that it is practically a household word.

For many years it was advertised in France with a running campaign in the Paris metro which said: 'Dubo, Dubon, Dubonnet', implying 'something good visually, something good tasting and the product itself'. It is made in two forms, red and white. The red is a mixture of red and white wines; the white is made from white wine only.

As was the case with so many alcoholic beverages during the nineteenth century, it was promoted as a tonic by its inventor, Joseph Dubonnet, and as such contained quinine (q.v.). The version now made in south-western France has a base of mistelles (wine the fermentation of which has been arrested by a dose of spirits), with herbs added. It is also made in other countries, like the U.S.A., under licence. The white version is now known as Dry Dubonnet.

DUTCH GIN

Known in its native land as genever (q.v.), this is the forerunner of our modern gin. According to most sources, the Dutch were the first people to make gin, some 400 years ago. They called it genever from the Dutch word for its main flavouring element, juniper. Genever was corrupted and shortened by its British enthusiasts into 'gin'.

EAU-DE-VIE

Spirit made from fermented and distilled juice of grapes or other fruit. The name literally means 'water of life', and is the French translation of the Latin, aqua vitae. Lost in the mists of history is the truth about when and where distilling, the basic method of producing eau-de-vie, was discovered. The chances are it was an Arab invention, used well before Mahomet ruled that alcohol should be shunned by his followers, that is, sometime before A.D. 600. The original 'water of life' was sharply alcoholic and soon began to have a second nickname — 'burning water', aqua ardens, or, as it is still known in some countries, aguardiente.

To render it less fiery, it was sugared; to make it even 'healthier', herbs and other flavours were added for their medicinal qualities and to impart different flavours. Thus, in all probability, liqueurs were born. (For individual flavours, see under the name of the flavouring agent — Fraises, Mûres, Mirabelle, etc.) Eau Clairette is one of the earliest known eaux-de-vie, made from alcohol with citrus flavouring, and probably sweetened with honey.

Many of the best eaux-de-vie are French, from Alsace or Lorraine. It should always be water-clear, and is usually allowed to age in bottle. Most eaux-de-vie (especially alcool blanc) should be drunk icy cold.

Germany, Switzerland and some East European lands also make delicious eaux-de-vie.
An eau-de-vie often used for cocktails is calvados:

> **HONEYMOON. Mix 1 fl oz each calvados, Bénédictine and lemon juice with a few drops of curaçao. Shake with ice.**

EGG LIQUEURS

See advocaat.

ELIXIR

The word means an alcohol in which certain flavours are dissolved, and came from the Arab word for the fabled philosopher's stone. By using an elixir the medieval alchemist was supposed to be able to change base metals into gold, or help men to live forever – eau-de-vie, in fact. Several words that begin with 'al' or 'el' have an Arabic origin, including 'al-cohol' itself, and 'al-chemy'.

Elixir d'Anvers is a Belgian herbal liqueur made from a maceration of spices, which is then distilled and sweetened. Elixir de China is an Italian liqueur with quinine; others include Elixir de Cola, de Garus, and de la Grande Chartreuse.

ENZIAN

The German word for gentian, a mountain plant the root of which is used frequently as one of the flavouring agents for liqueurs. Enzian, as a liqueur name, is found mainly in Germany and Switzerland. In France the main gentian brand is Suze Liqueur.

ERDBEERGEIST

The German name for a distillation of strawberries with added alcohol. Its taste is similar to the French eau-de-vie de fraises. (Soft fruit does not produce enough alcohol naturally to preserve it. Thus alcohol is added and the fruit and alcohol are distilled together.)

FALERNUM

A famous wine from Campania in the Naples area, popular during the Roman Empire for some 300 years. It had as good a reputation in its day as that of Clos de Vougeot today. It was a wine of breeding that would last, historians say, 'for many decades', before reaching its zenith, dark red and alcoholic. Latin writers from Horace and Pliny to Martial and Galen sang its praises. A liqueur called Falernum is still made in Italy.

FENNEL

One of the herbs once used in the manufacture of absinthe, with a taste similar to anis.

FERNET BRANCA

An Italian bitters and digestif, made since 1845, now licensed to be made in several countries (U.S.A., France, Switzerland and Argentina) and exported round the world. It is made with 30 different herbs, including Chinese rhubarb and ginger, steeped in old white wine and brandy, and aged for at least a year in casks. It makes no health-giving claims, though its taste is highly medicinal, to say the least. Widely used to aid digestion, the Italians never use it as a hangover cure (they use sugarless espresso coffee for that).

*Branca-menta is perhaps a more palatable version,
with a pleasant semi-bitter flavour, which is usually
drunk as a Highball with soda water.*

FIG BRANDY

*Even teetotal Arab states (and don't forget the Arabs
invented distilling) make spirits, despite their Moslem
principles. Tunisia, for example, has two: fig brandy
called Boukha, and a spirit-based date liqueur called
Tibarine. The Germans also make a fig liqueur.*

FINE, FINE-A-L'EAU

*In France you may hear people ordering 'une fine'
(pronounced 'feen') and that is supposed to bring
them a cognac fine champagne, the top grade of
cognac. Often, however, what they get is simply a
good brandy. Fine-a-l'eau is a brandy Highball, usually
made with plain water.*

FINNISH LIQUEURS

*The Finns have some unusual liqueurs made from
Arctic plants, from which they also make jams and
jellies. One popular liqueur there is called Lakka, a
bitter-sweet compounding or maceration of cloud-
berries. They also have Mesimarja made from arctic
bramble, and Happonia from ligon berries.*

FIOR D'ALPI

*Herbs and flowers from the Italian Alps go into this
pale yellow liqueur. It is sold in tall bottles with a
sugar-encrusted twig in each one.*

FLAVOURINGS

*Flavours and aromas are added to spirits to make
liqueurs by distilling herbs or other aromatic agents.
Usually the herb, bark, flower, grain, or whatever is*

used for flavouring, must be dampened or macerated in water or in alcohol before it can be heated to the point where its aroma will be transferred in the form of steam. The steam, once condensed back into liquid, will have a concentrated flavour of the ingredient used. This concentrate may then be added to another spirit, either pure alcohol, or some already flavoured spirit, like rum, whisky, or gin. Flavour can also be imparted by a cold infusion of fruits or herbs; maceration in alcohol, or percolation (passing them through the flavouring agent as you do to make coffee). You can make your own liqueur by simply steeping lemon peel, say, or a chilli pepper, in a relatively pure alcohol like vodka for a few days.

*F*ORBIDDEN FRUIT
Whisky-based, American citrus liqueur that used to be made from grapefruit, with honey and orange.

*F*RAISES, Eau-de-vie de
A sweet liqueur, eau-de-vie de fraises is a distilled spirit or fruit brandy made from strawberries (Erdbeergeist in Germany), which is usually clear, water-white. The French make many such eaux-de-vie: framboise (raspberry), mûre (blackberry), kirsch (cherry) and so on. (See also *fruit brandy*.)

*F*RAMBOISES, Eau-de-vie de
Usually, like eau-de-vie de fraises, a pure white spirit but made from raspberries, not strawberries.

*F*RANCE
France boasts one of the world's largest assortments of liqueurs and spirits, including fruit, herb, spice and nut liqueurs, brandies and white alcohols. Over 80 million bottles of French-made liqueurs are exported annually, and over 20 million bottles are made abroad

under licence. Makers include Rocher Frères, Dolfi,
Reynier, Cusenier, Bardinet and Marie Brizard, not to
mention specific cognacs, vermouths and famous
digestifs like Chartreuse, Cointreau and Bénédictine.

FRUIT BRANDY

What the French call eau-de-vie — colourless but
aromatic and powerfully alcoholic. Fruit brandy is a
distillation of the fermented juice of grapes or other
fruit, often with crushed pips as well as the flesh. Some
so-called fruit brandies, such as cherry, peach or
apricot, are not true distillations, but macerations of
the fruit in alcohol; these are not really brandy at all.

FRUIT LIQUEURS

The fruits most commonly used in liqueur-making are
probably the citrus family. There are dozens of good
citrus liqueurs, ranging from Cointreau, Grand
Marnier and curaçao (q.v.) to Van der Hum,
Mandarine and the Greek Kitron. Cherry liqueurs are
also popular, especially in northern Europe. Mara-
schino is an Italian version. Blackcurrants are used to
make cassis, which originates in Dijon. Apricot and
peach liqueurs are also fairly common. Fruit liqueurs
made by maceration are sometimes called cordials in
the U.S.A. In the U.K. cordials are likely to be low- or
non-alcoholic beverages.

GALLIANO

A golden Italian contribution to the liqueur kingdom, and one more to add to the 'secret formula' brigade, the ingredients of which are passed, alliteratively, through 'fossil filters' to keep it pure. It is made with over 30 herbs, roots, berries and flowers steeped and distilled into an essence which is then blended with spirits, to give a strength of around 35%. It was named after an Italian officer who, in 1895, resisted a siege at Enda Jesus in Abyssinia for 44 days. Eventually the Italian government of the time ordered him to surrender to superior forces.

Today the liqueur is best known outside Italy as the base for a cocktail, the Harvey Wallbanger. According to the manufacturers, Harvey was a surfer from California who enjoyed celebrating his achievements with his favourite beverage (see below). Like other liqueurs, Galliano may also be used in cooking, to flavour a batter for prawns (scampi), for example.

HARVEY WALLBANGER is half a measure of Galliano floating on top of that well-established favourite, the Screwdriver – four measures of orange juice, half a measure of vodka.

GARNIER

Company name of one of the biggest producers of liqueurs in France, with a very large selection headed

by the cumin-flavoured clear spirit 'Liqueur d'Or' (gold water) with golden specks floating in it. (See also *danziger goldwasser*.)

GAY-LUSSAC

Joseph Gay-Lussac was a French chemist who died in 1850. He invented, and gave his name to, a system for measuring the alcoholic strength of wines, liqueurs and spirits as a percentage of their volume. The system is being replaced by one known as the O.I.M.L. system, based on the same principles but modernized to make it more accurate. Wines are likely to contain from 8.5% of alcohol up to 13 or 14%. Sherries have about 17% alcohol, vermouths 15%, and ports 18-20%; while liqueurs and spirits can vary in strength anywhere from 17% alcohol for some of the new 'low-strength' liqueurs like Irish Creams, up to 28% for Malibu and Cocoribe, 38% for Grand Marnier, 40% for gin, and as high as 45% or more for whiskies. 'Proof' is an old and complicated system for alcohol measurement that is gradually disappearing from regular usage.

GEIST

German for a liqueur made by macerating soft fruit, such as raspberries (Himbeergeist), strawberries (Erdbeergeist) or blackberries (Brombeergeist) in alcohol and then distilling them. The French equivalent is Eau-de-vie (q.v.).

GENEVER

In Dutch, this word means juniper, and is used to describe Holland's gin because juniper is one of the principal ingredients with which it is flavoured. Dutch gin is supposed to be drunk straight and icy cold. It is difficult to combine it with other tastes into a reasonably drinkable cocktail because it is distilled from a malted cereal mash that gives it a distinctive

flavour. Jonge *(young)* Genever *is white and 'light',
while* Oude *(old)* Genever *has a yellowish tinge, the
'heaviness' of the latter being due to the higher
proportion of 'malt wine', made from a mixture of rye,
barley and corn (maize).*

GENTIAN

One of the root flavourings used for many liqueurs,
and a very bitter one. A French version, popular in
France, is Suze Liqueur. In Paris, shortly after the
Liberation, the bar of the Scribe Hotel, where all
newspapermen were put up, could offer nothing but
Suze to the thirsty journalists, most of whom managed
to resist its cure-all reputation in favour of the less
medicinal pleasures of PX store supplies of American
whiskey. It is widely advertised and sold in France (but,
curiously, I have never heard anyone order it in a bar).
The German version, Enzian, tastes equally medicinal.

GERMAN BRANDY

One of the best of non-French brandies is Asbach
Uralt, which is distilled at Rüdesheim.

GERMAN GIN

The Germans make gins with a much stronger flavour
of juniper than English and American versions.
Steinhäger is one, distilled from a mash of wheat,
barley and juniper berries. Schinkenhäger (38%
alcohol) is similar. Wacholder is made from neutral
spirits, juniper flavoured.

GERMAN LIQUEURS

Germany produces a large selection of liqueurs with
various spirit bases and flavourings. Jägermeister, with
56 herbs and 35% of alcohol is bittersweet and widely
distributed; Jambo Salato is made from passion fruit,
blended with 25% of alcohol; Hazelnut (Haselnüss

mit Ei) is a mixture of nuts with eggs. The gentian liqueur made in Bavaria is Enzian, another bitters. Bonifactius Korn contains coriander, carnation flavouring, mint and peppermint. German Kümmel has the flavour of cumin and is very similar to the Scandinavian types. Germans seem to like their liqueurs either very sweet or very dry and bitter. There is a tendency to place all these beverages under the umbrella term 'schnapps'.

G^{IN}

The parent of what you and I mix with our tonic was Holland Genever (the word is Dutch for juniper), made by distilling grain spirits and a mash of juniper and things like cassia bark, coriander seed, angelica root and other esoteric ingredients. Each maker has his own secret formula.

*E*nglish gin is less powerfully perfumed. It comes in several varieties. The London type uses much the same ingredients as Holland gin. Some London gin is as clear as water, while some is straw-coloured from being matured in oak casks. Examples are Gilbey's, Gordon's, Beefeater and Booth's. Plymouth gin (made in Plymouth, England) has a different flavour from London gins.

*G*in was once the bad boy of the spirits world. While most drinks can boast an historical association of some distinction (sherry and Grandees of Spain, rum and buccaneers, whisky and Scottish lairds), gin became a sort of eighteenth-century tranquillizer, which was cheap, abundant and potent, and helped take people's minds off the miserable social conditions. Taxes on gin were so light that even the poorest people could buy it. You could get 'dead drunk for tuppence,' they said, and unlicensed dram shops opened everywhere. In 1733, in a London far smaller than it is today, there were nearly 7,000 of them.

*G*eorge II's parliament decided to end illegal sales of uncontrolled gin. Even so it was still the easiest and cheapest way for the populace to forget its woes, and it was not until the latter part of Victoria's reign that these abuses gradually stopped. Gin began to be accepted in polite society.

During the jazz age it climbed to complete respectability 'up the stem of the cocktail glass', as Anthony Hogg, a British expert, puts it. The Dry Martini is one of the most popular aperitifs in the world and gin and tonic one of the simplest and most favoured long drinks. If you are a stickler for perfection, here is the modern ceremonial way to make your Dry Martini.

Put a tall jug filled with ice into the refrigerator along with the cocktail glasses. When they are good and cold, remove them from the refrigerator and discard the ice. Add a few fresh ice cubes, then five to ten parts of gin, depending on how dry you like it, and one of dry vermouth. Stir quickly and thoroughly. Strain into the glasses. Then, either drink it as it is, or twist a sliver of lemon peel over the glass (never, say connoisseurs, drop the peel in), so the lemon's aromatic oil floats on top. Or you can add an olive.

If you have made more than you need, remove the ice from the jug and keep what's left in the refrigerator for further attention. A Gibson is the same thing with a pickled onion instead of the lemon or olive.

White Italian vermouth tends to be slightly less dry than French. A real fanatic pours the vermouth over the ice, drains it and then pours the gin on the aromatic ice. A dash of Pernod adds a certain exotic quality to the drink, but then it is no longer a Martini.

Recipes for gin drinks abound. There are gin slings, and rickeys, and Collinses and flips and fizzes galore. I rather like the Solid Pink Gin made by my friend Eve Dosch. This unusual dish is prepared by flavouring plain gelatine with Pink Gin.

SOLID PINK GIN. Make the gelatine according to the directions on the packet, but replace the water with the same amount of gin, slightly diluted with 4-5 dashes of Angostura bitters. Serve it like a jellied consommé, cold, with half a lemon to squeeze over it.

The romantic **ALEXANDER** is two parts dry gin, one part each crème de cacao and cream, shaken thoroughly with cracked ice, and strained into a glass. (Others say it is one part brandy, one part crème de cacao and one part cream.)

ORANGE FIZZ. Use two parts gin, one of orange juice and half each of lemon and lime juice. Shake with ice and add a dash of Pernod. Mix half and half with soda water.

WHITE LADY. Mix gin and lemon juice in equal quantities with a dash of Cointreau and sugar to taste, all well shaken with the white of an egg and ice.

GINGER LIQUEURS

According to Bruce Cost's study Ginger Here & There, ginger itself was a panacea in the Far East in earliest times, several thousand years B.C. It was one of the exotic products carried across the Gobi desert by camel caravans well before Marco Polo's day, to ancient Greece, and Imperial Rome, and finally throughout Europe in the Dark Ages. Even today, tons of ginger are imported into the U.S.A. and the U.K. for their ginger-loving Chinese populations. It was known especially as a cure for nausea, for colds and for flatulence. In fact, according to tests in the U.S.A., it is more effective than dramamine for seasickness. The Chinese say it is 'yang', or hot and warming.

Ginger liqueurs (also known as ginger wines) are still made in England. If you want to pay for it, or are a member of a royal family, you can have a special ginger liqueur made up for you. King Edward VII's doctor asked the famed London wine firm Berry Bros & Rudd, whose shop on St. James's Street has hardly changed in 150 years, to 'produce something warming for his majesty to take after his winter morning's drive in his new motor car'. So they did, and the result did the trick for the king. Spicy King's Ginger Liqueur is still an excellent stimulant on a cold night. Royal Ginger-Chocolate and Leroux's Ginger Flavoured Brandy are other ginger spirits.

GLAYVA

A whisky-based concoction flavoured with herbs, a whiff of orange and heather honey, first made in the late 1940s in Midlothian, Scotland. The label bears a Moor's head emblem, supposedly to commemorate a certain 16-year-old Scot, named Borthwick. This young man, having slain a Saracen chieftain in unsuccessful defence of Robert the Bruce, rescued the King's heart, put the Saracen's head on a spear, and triumphantly brought both back to Scotland.

G*LEN*

A favourite prefix in the names of Scotch whiskies, associated with the location of the distillery – among them Glenlivet, Glen Grant, Glenmorangie, Glenugie and Glenfiddich – see **whisky** for the reason why.

G*OLDWASSER*

A clear liqueur containing minute specks of gold and flavoured with cumin or caraway for digestion and with aniseed against the evil eye. Arnaldo de Villanova, a thirteenth-century Spanish Catalan alchemist (or doctor), is said to have saved the Pope's life with an elixir of herbs and spirits, flecked with gold-leaf. The Holy Father was so pleased that he absolved Villanova from Torquemada's Inquisitional third degree.

G*ORNY DUBNYA*

Russia produces some liqueurs, most of them with a vodka base, some with a wine base. This bitter one contains ginger, angelica and cloves among other flavourings.

G*RAND MARNIER*

One of the 'greats' of the liqueur world is Grand Marnier Lapostole. The 'apostle' in its name has nothing to do with religion; it is the name of a family who began making liqueurs in 1827.

*T*wo generations later, Louis-Alexander Marnier-Lapostole, a grandson-in-law of the firm's founder, and a travelling salesman, took a round-the-world trip on which he discovered Haitian oranges. Combining

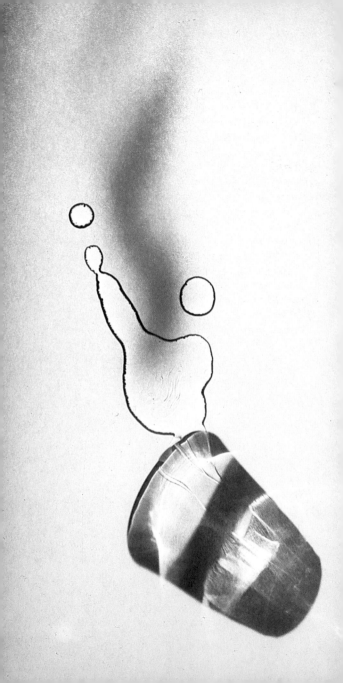

their bitterness with fine cognac brandy was his idea.
Today the juice of wild Caribbean oranges is blended
with brandy at the Grand Marnier château near
Cognac, France, then taken to the distillery at
Nauphle-le-Château, not far from Paris. At Nauphle
the orange juice and cognac are redistilled, blended
with sugar and other aromatics and aged in oak.
Grand Marnier's success lies partly in the energetic
way it is promoted. At the famous Le Mans 24 Hour
auto races, for example, the firm keeps a crêpe stand
open night and day. These delicious crêpes are two
feet across and sprinkled with Grand Marnier from a
huge bottle, then folded into quarters for all and
sundry to enjoy. Crêpe demonstrations like this are put
on all over Europe, and even occasionally in the U.S.A.
(In Palermo, Sicily, alone, two chefs turned out some
3,000 crêpes a day each at a recent exhibition). The
U.S.A. is Grand Marnier's biggest market in
quantity, but Belgium uses more of it per capita.
Grand Marnier is an essential element in a good duck
à l'orange, a sweet soufflé or a flambéed omelette.
For a dynamite cocktail:

Stir 1 fl oz vodka and ½ fl oz Grand Marnier with 2 fl oz black coffee and a dash of crème de menthe. Add ice and decorate with a sprig of fresh mint.

GRAPE BRANDY

Perhaps the most common type of brandy made
throughout the world. Practically every wine-pro-
ducing country uses some of its grape juice for
brandy-making. The most famed for flavour are the
French cognacs and armagnacs, but huge quantities
are made in Italy, Germany, Spain, Portugal, the
U.S.A., Australia, Russia, and the South American
wine-producing countries of Argentina, Peru and
Chile. The two latter produce a very aromatic wine
brandy from muscat grapes, called Pisco. This is the
basis of Pisco Sour, a truly excellent drink.

PISCO SOUR. Mix 2 fl oz Pisco brandy and 1 teaspoon fresh lime juice with sugar to taste. Shake with egg white to fluff it up, and add 3 or 4 ice cubes.

GRAPEFRUIT LIQUEUR

The Dutch, ever inventive when it comes to liqueurs, have produced Paradis from grapefruit juice and neutral spirits. Except for its effect on your own spirits, you might think this was mere sweetened grapefruit juice. It is made by the same firm whose beers are consumed worldwide, Heineken.

GRAPPA

A fire-water brandy made in Italy from the left-over skins of grapes that have been relieved of their juices in the making of wine. It is a cousin of the similar French product, marc, the Portuguese bagaciera and Spanish aguardiente. Such brandies are usually cheaper than those made from wine itself, less smooth, and need a fairly hardy constitution to take as a regular beverage. Properly aged in wood, however, they can be good.

GRENADINE

A non-alcoholic pomegranate-flavoured sweet syrup used in various cocktails.

GROG

A British admiral of the early eighteenth century named Vernon, who used to wear a grosgrain coat, and was therefore nicknamed 'Old Grog', is responsible for this nickname for rum, and rum-based mixed drinks. He would give his crews slightly sugared rum, mixed with hot water, to make them more willing to face the enemy. This mixture became known as 'grog'. Even today grogs are usually wintry, hot drinks – like American Grog, which consists of 1 fl oz dark Jamaican rum, a clove, the juice of half a lemon and 1 cinnamon stick poured into a heated glass or mug and filled with boiling water.

HALLGARTEN, House of

One of England's foremost importers of liqueurs, known mainly for their 'Royal' line. Their invention and flagship is Royal Mint-Chocolate Liqueur, a creamy mixture with a predominantly chocolate flavour.

HEERING, PETER

A Danish house famous for its cherry brandy, patriotically using only Danish cherries. Their brandy used to be called Cherry Heering, until too many imitators began making similar liqueurs. The firm also produces schnapps and aquavit, and makes Kahlúa for Europe under licence from its Mexican inventors.

HERBAL WINES

The forerunners of today's vermouths and many liqueurs were concocted from wine and herbs by medieval monks. Mainly medicinal in purpose, they consisted of herbs steeped in wine – strictly speaking not liqueurs, but flavoured wine.

HIMBEERGEIST

It takes about sixty pounds of wild raspberries to make a single litre bottle of this delectable German spirit. The fruit is first macerated in alcohol, then distilled. The French name for a similar liqueur (though theirs is usually clear white) is eau-de-vie de framboises. Both can be used in a 'Kir' as an alternative to cassis: pour a few drops in the bottom of a wine glass, then fill up with cold dry white wine.

HIPPOCRAS

The same famous Greek physician who proposed the Hippocratic oath for doctors also helped invent this ancient form of vermouth – spicy wine that was filtered through a bag of his design. An early type of iced drink, it was still in favour through the 1700s.

The novelist Norman Douglas of Capri fame claimed it was an 'unrivalled stimulant'. His recipe included a bottle of Burgundy, 1 oz crushed cinnamon, 2 lb icing sugar, 1 oz ginger, ¼ oz vanilla and ¼ oz cloves. (Mr Douglas is not very informative about what to do next, but I imagine the mixture is steeped for a week, the bottle tightly corked, then drunk just before you hope it will affect you!)

HOMEMADE LIQUEURS

During the days of Prohibition in the U.S.A., many a householder made his own herbal wines and liqueurs, mainly to hide the fairly rough taste of available alcohol. In many European countries where fruit is plentiful, liqueurs have been made at home for generations. Apricots, peaches and plums are favourite fruits for such treatment; first a mash is made of the fruit and its juice, the kernels cracked to give a bitter bite, and the lot marinated in alcohol. Other fruit too, like sloes or blackberries, can be used. An amusing book on the subject is Wine Man's Bluff, by Phoebe Hitchens, containing instructions for making a variety of potations with fruits and flowers.

In Germany, particularly, homemade liqueurs are a normal part of any household's culinary practice. In a German cookbook by Henriette David, published in

1844 and still in use, some 15 such recipes are given for carnation flower, cinnamon, herb, and other liqueurs, along with everyday recipes like those for stews and game and sweets. The French, too, make a great variety of liqueurs at home, mainly by macerating fruit in alcohol. In fact, you can turn vodka into all sorts of 'liqueurs' simply by steeping herbs, fruit, lemon peel or chillies in it.

HONEY

One of the earliest of liqueurs was 'honey wine', or mead, made from fermented honey and spices. It was very popular in almost prehistoric days in the cold north, where grapes did not grow but honey was available. Scandinavian myth has it that the supreme deity, Odin, brought this boon to man. Disguised as a worm(!) he crept into an enormous cave where the formula was brewed. Once within he resumed his godlike splendour and seduced the cave's guardian, a lovely blonde giantess. He begged from her a sip of the mead she was protecting from such creatures as he; she agreed. The divine thief drank her whole supply in one mouthful, transformed himself into a mighty eagle, and flew back to civilization. (They had rather vivid imaginations in those days.)

HYDROMEL

According to no less an authority than Alexandre Dumas, hydromel was the most popular libation throughout the ancient world. His recipe was to put one part of honey into three parts of water and set it in the sun to ferment. 'It tastes good and fortifies the stomach,' he says, and adds that it was 'as strong as Spanish wine'. A similar potion is still in use in Russia, Poland and Ethiopia!

IJK

INFUSION

A method of making liqueurs by steeping the flavouring elements – flowers, herbs, fruit, seeds – in alcohol, or letting the alcohol seep through them (as in percolating coffee). This method is used when flavours are so delicate that they may be harmed by distillation.

IRISH CREAM LIQUEURS

First introduced in 1975, a new group of liqueurs made with Irish whiskey, blended with other spirits and Irish cream. Some contain chocolate, coffee or honey as well as cream. Sticklers for tradition object that these are not strictly liqueurs but after-dinner drinks, although this seems to have no effect on their popularity.

IRISH WHISKEY

Irish whiskey differs from Scotch in several ways: 1. It is spelt with an 'e'. 2. In malting, the damp barley is dried to stop sprouting by heat, but not peat. 3. Its mash usually contains unmalted barley. 4. It is triple-distilled. 5. It usually has more malted alcohol than grain alcohol. 6. It is often aged for 10 to 15 years. The Irish Distillers Group has managed the industry since 1966.

IVY

Believe it or not, certain types of ivy leaves are used for flavouring in some liqueurs. (Don't make a mistake and use poison ivy instead!)

IZARRA

An armagnac-based liqueur from the Basque country of France. Its name means 'star' in the Basque dialect. Like Chartreuse, it comes in two versions and strengths: the yellow has 32 different herbs in it, and 43% of alcohol; the green has more herbs, 48 types, and is stronger with 55% of alcohol. The herbs gathered in the Pyrenees Mountains are blended and distilled with the brandy, then aged in wood.

JAEGERMEISTER (Jägermeister)

A German herb liqueur, dark red and appreciated by hunters, if its name is any indication. (The name means 'master of the hunt' in German.)

JIGGER

A measure used by barmen, usually 1½ fluid ounces, which is considered a fair portion of spirit to serve. I prefer to serve 2 fluid ounces per person for individual servings. Most liqueur glasses hold only about 1 fluid ounce, as do some miniature bottles of spirits.

JUNIPER

A purplish, pungent berry used for flavouring liqueurs and spirits. In most gins, for example, the predominant flavour is usually juniper. The shrub it comes from is a type of evergreen.

KAHLÚA

Mexico's contribution to the liqueur world – a rich coffee-based, sweet affair, made in Mexico with

Mexican coffee beans for the Eastern Hemisphere, and licensed to Denmark's Peter Heering for production in Europe.

BLACKEYED SUSAN. This requires 2 fl oz vodka, 1 fl oz Kahlúa and a dash of lemon. Pour over ice.

MOKKAIS. Blend 2 fl oz Kahlúa and 1 fl oz Pippermint Get. Shake with ice.

KIRSCH (Kirschwasser)

True eau-de-vie, or brandy, made from cherries. Kirsch is the German word for cherry, but the same word is used in France for the clear, strong, white cherry brandy so popular in Europe for after-dinner sipping, though it is far from sweet. It has a lovely aroma of cherry, and a sharp, almost bitter alcoholic flavour. Kirsch is made by including the crushed cherry kernels with the juice of the fruit when it is distilled. In olden days, most kirsch was made from wild cherries, which gave it a more pungent flavour, almost like biting into the fresh fruit. In Germany, kirschwasser, or kirsch, is often included under the general term schnapps. The best German versions come from the Black Forest, while the best French ones are made in Alsace. The Swiss and Austrians also make excellent kirsch. Black cherries are always used, picked in some of the sheltered valleys of central Europe.

KITRON

The Greeks make this liqueur by distilling their grape brandy with lemon leaves and sweetening the result.

KORN

A type of low-strength brandy, somewhat similar to American whiskey but made in Germany from corn (maize), and found in most German-speaking countries. Some of it is flavoured with juniper, and some is bottled as Doppelkorn, a strong version with 38% of alcohol. Well-known brands are Doornkaat and Furst Bismarck. Both are considered varieties of schnapps.

KSARA

Even Libya makes small quantities of spirits. One is Ksara, an anis-flavoured arrack (q.v.), made from wine.

KÜMMEL

A distilled pure grain spirit, much like vodka, but flavoured with fresh caraway or cumin seeds. Various brands claim to be the original kümmel (which reminds me of the three restaurants on New York's Third Avenue, nearly side by side, and each proclaiming itself as 'The Original Joe's'). One story is that it originated in the Middle Ages in the Netherlands. When Peter the Great of Russia was learning about ship-building in Holland in 1696, he apparently also learned to drink kümmel and took the formula back with him to Russia. Another story is that Evan Lucas Bols pressed the formula upon the Tsar. In any case, Riga, in Latvia, became the famed centre for kümmel before World War I. Some of the names made famous then moved out of Russia after the revolution. Mentzendorff is now made in Holland, Wolfschmidt moved to Denmark and Gilka is made in Berlin. There are dozens of different brands being made today in Europe and the U.S.A.

KUMQUAT

A curaçao type of liqueur made from this small, oval-shaped citrus fruit is produced on the Greek island of Corfu.

L EMON

One of the citrus fruits whose dried peel or leaves are often used for liqueurs. Depending on nationality, their labels may say citron or Zitronen or whatever the local name for lemon is. The type of lemon usually used is the bergamot, whose peel can also be distilled into perfume. The Greek lemon liqueur is called Kitron, a Corsican one is Cedratine and an Austrian variety is Kaiserbirn.

L ILLET

A French, light vermouth made with wine from the Bordeaux vineyards, in which fruit peels and herbs are steeped before it is aged in oak. It can be either red or white and has a slightly bitter orange flavour.

L INIE

A famous aquavit from Norway, pale gold in colour, and smooth as a sea-voyage can make it. It is aged in oaken casks that are shipped to Australia and back before their contents are bottled. The changing temperatures it passes through, as it crosses the 'line' (the Equator) twice, not to mention the thorough mixing it gets from the ship's motion en route, make it deliciously unique, aromatic and powerful.

LIQUEUR

The word means a flavoured spirit, usually sweet, which can be based on grain alcohol, brandy, whisky, rum, vodka, or any other pure alcohol. The flavouring can be of fruit, herbs, nuts, seeds or a mixture of several such things, either by distillation, infusion or maceration, or by adding essential oils.

LIQUEUR DE FRAMBOISES

A red raspberry liqueur is now being made and used, rather as cassis is, with white wine, to make an aperitif like Kir. It is delicious poured over raspberry sorbet.

LIQUEUR DES MOINES

A fine herbal mixture with a cognac base. The name means 'liquor of the monks'.

LONDON GIN

*Not necessarily any longer made in or near London, this is what might be called a generic 'everyday' type of gin – dry, and flavoured with various 'secret' blends of herbs to give different brands slightly different flavours. London-type gin has a milder flavour than Dutch or German gins, and is made all over the world from Japan to the U.S.A. (See also **gin**.)*

M

MACERATION

In liqueur terms, this means to steep a flavouring agent – such as fruit, herbs, flower petals – in alcohol so that it breaks down and imparts its flavour to the alcohol.

MALT WHISKY

The 'original' whisky from Scotland was always made from an entirely malt mash. The barley grains were and still are dampened and allowed to sprout, a natural process that causes the barley to change its starchy content into sugar. When this process has advanced as far as the distillery wishes, it is stopped by heating the malted barley over peat fires, which contributes additional flavour. Water is added and the barley is allowed to ferment into a sort of beer. This beer is then distilled to make raw whisky, a white alcohol, which is then redistilled to produce whisky that needs careful ageing in wood to cause it to take on colour. Most of it is then sold for blending, before it is bottled. A little, after ageing, is sold as malt, or single malt, whisky.

There was a tremendous fuss made when it was first suggested, around the turn of the century, that malt whisky be blended with grain whisky to make what 90 per cent of drinkers today know as Scotch. Before this practice became widespread, consumption of whisky was only a fraction of what it is today.

MANDARINE

A brandy-based liqueur, among the best known of which is Mandarine Napoléon. Made in Belgium, this potent aperitif is flavoured with a distillate of Spanish mandarines, the peel of which is first soaked in cognac, then redistilled. Sugar is added, and the mixture matured for six months to become a light, dryish type of curaçao. Similar liqueurs are made in France and Holland.

MARASCHINO

Since 1779, this cherry liqueur, originally from Dalmatia, Yugoslavia, has been made in Italy from a special sour, red cherry, called marasca in Italian. Crushed kernels and sweetening agents are added to the cherry juice. The whole is then distilled three times, and kept in glass containers. The liqueur is clear white, and has a powerfully nutty, cherry flavour. Italian makers include Stock, Luxardo, Dolfi and, oldest of all, Drioli. Maraschino is often used as a condiment in cooking, and in cocktail-making.

MARC

The French term for a brandy made from the residue of grape skins and stalks and seeds (pomace) left over after the grapes have been pressed to make wine. This kind of brandy is also called grappa, bagaciera, or aguardiente in Italy, Portugal, and Spain respectively. It is often a very raw drink, very alcoholic, very 'down-market' compared to wine brandy. A good French version is marc de Bourgogne, which can be a pleasant drink.

MARTINI VERMOUTH

This famed vermouth, today known as an ingredient for the Martini Cocktail, has been around, in various forms, for over 100 years. Originally the Martini Cocktail was made with gin and sweet red vermouth.

Gradually things changed, so that an American cookbook of the 1920s was advising a half gin, half white vermouth Martini. Today, the Martini is more likely to be eight or ten parts gin to one of white Martini. Whatever the formula, Martini is one of the best-known names in the vermouth world, whether as a straight drink or with soda (as is often the case in Europe), or in cocktails.

MASTIKA

A Greek liqueur made with anis and herb mastika (resin) as flavouring. It is sweet and milky white. Mastika from the island of Chios is considered the best of anis drinks by the Greeks. Ouzo (q.v.) is another.

MEAD

An ancient 'liqueur', usually homemade with various combinations of honey, fermented with malt, spices, yeast and water. In American colonial days it was known as 'metheglin'. A honey-sweet mead is still made today but is probably nothing like the original.

MENTHE, Crème de

The greatest of after-dinner liqueurs, in my opinion. Poured over crushed ice in either green or white versions, as a Crème de Menthe Frappée, it is the most refreshing, mouth-reviving drink I know. Perhaps I am influenced by the long, delightful hours with that wasp-waisted bottle of Pippermint Get, sitting on our honeymoon balcony as we sipped and waited for the sun to sink slowly across Palamos bay. (It was a long wait. The bay faced east, but by then we didn't notice.) It packs a punch that is not in the least feminine. Other good brands include Freezomint, Marie Brizard and Giffard from France. Most other liqueur-producing countries – Italy, Mexico, Spain, and the U.S.A. – have their own variations. Mint is supposed to be good for the digestion, if you need an excuse for drinking it.

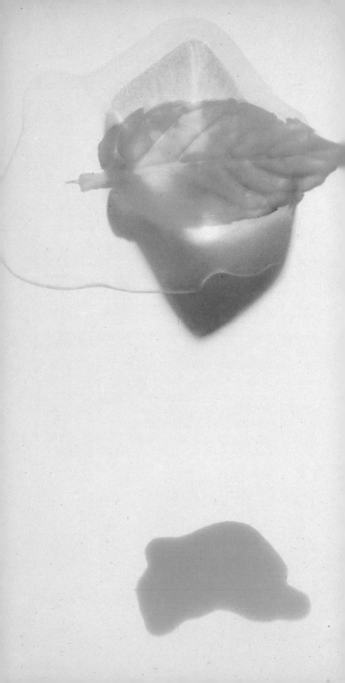

MERSIN

You might not think Turkey would produce much in the way of liqueurs, but Mersin proves you mistaken. This orange-flavoured drink is to be taken along with a cup or two of excellent Turkish coffee, strong and black. An experience that can be as mesmerizing as watching the dervishes whirl.

METAXAS

The most famous Greek brandy, rather heavier than French, and with a slightly sweeter taste. It is made in several qualities from muscat grape wines, and aged in tarred barrels, they say.

MEZCAL

The second stage in the making of tequila. The first stage is the basic juice of the agave cactus, called pulque, which can be drunk, fermented, as a type of beer. Pulque is also distilled into a brandy called mezcal, and mezcal is further distilled to give the finer grade, tequila. All three stages are alcoholic drinks, and can be consumed as such, but tequila is by far the purest and most palatable of the three. Mezcal, the middle stage, is often bottled with an agave-worm in it. (This is said to give the drinker courage. It certainly takes courage to drink it!)

MIDORI

A relative newcomer to the liqueur world, this is a Japanese concoction made from the flesh of melons. Its pale green tinge ('midori' is Japanese for green) is added to it. A very sweet, very green drink, and with not much melon flavour.

MIRABELLE

This is a pure-white distillation of tiny yellowy-green plums, and one of France's best fruit brandies (an

Crème de menthe

alcool blanc). It is not at all sweet, but rather explosively sharp with a tremendous fruity aroma. It is not matured in wood, but in glass carboys. The German equivalent, quetsch, is more like a crème, made from Black Forest plums, fermented with selected yeasts and double-distilled, then aged in wood.

MOKKA (Mocha), Crème de

A type of coffee liqueur. Practically any country with a coffee industry – Mexico, Brazil, Turkey – makes some, and so do some places with a whisky industry – Ireland, Scotland, the U.S.A. – in imitation of the Irishman who started it all, with Irish coffee, at Shannon airport, back in the days when all transatlantic flights had to stop over there for refuelling. But true Crème de Mokka was a German invention, known well before World War II. Theoretically, mocha should be made with Arabian mocha coffee.

MÛRES, Crème de

A French liqueur made from wild blackberries.

MYRTILLES, Crème de

A liqueur made from crushed wild bilberries or myrtles from the Ardèche and Drôme valleys. The myrtle plant was once sacred to Venus, and it was a token of resurrection. The berries are used in several liqueurs.

N/O

NAPOLEON BRANDY

Not as old as its name implies; the Napoleon referred to here (though the ads and bottles usually show a figure with his right hand thrust across his chest into his coat) is Napoleon III, known as Louis Napoleon, a mildly left-wing Emperor, who took power only in 1852 and managed to stay until he was deposed in 1870. As a refugee in London for two years, Prince Louis used to buy his wines and spirits from Berry Bros. & Rudd (still doing business on St James's Street, London). In their cellars, Louis Napoleon met secretly with colleagues to plot his return to power. Part of the cellars is still known as 'Napoleon's Corner'.

NOCINO

An Italian nut liqueur, made from walnuts steeped in brandy or a neutral spirit.

NOISETTE

A French liqueur made from hazelnuts.

NOIX, Crème de

A liqueur made in south-western France from walnuts, usually fresh green ones, and honey. It is

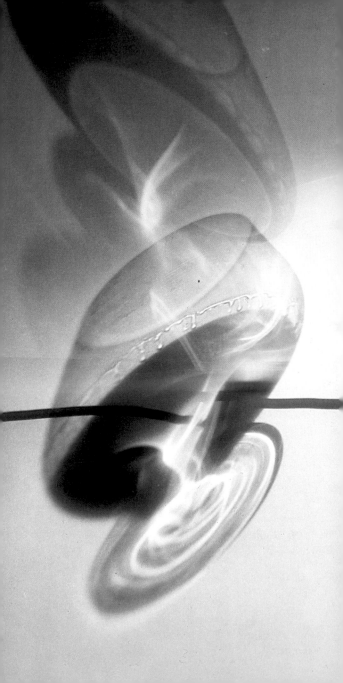

often called a *brou de noix* or *eau-de-vie de noix*, if it
has been distilled. (This region has a wonderful way
with its marvellous prunes; steeped whole, in brandy,
they beat all those childhood school-dinner prunes
into a cocked hat.)

*N*OYAU
A liqueur made usually from the kernels of peaches or
apricots, though sometimes of plums or cherries, with
a flavour like almonds.

*O*JEN
A type of pastis made in Spain in the town of Ojen
(pronounced 'ohen'). It is clear until mixed with water,
when it becomes milky. It has an aniseed or liquorice
flavour, and is made in both sweet and dry types.

*O*KE (Okolehao)
The nickname for Hawaii's contribution to liqueurs. It
is made, somewhat like tequila, from the root of the
ti plant, a tree that used to be sacred when Hawaii was
first visited by Western explorers. A type of ti-plant
beer was indigenous, but an early shipwrecked adven-
turer decided to distil the beer, using the redundant
cooler from his ship's cannon as a condenser. Today
oke is made in modern continuous stills.

*O*RANGE BITTERS
A stimulating bitters made from the peel of bitter
oranges, and not quite as astringent as those made
with quinine. Especially agreeable with orange drinks.

*O*RANGE LIQUEURS
One of the first orange liqueurs was triple-sec, which
is still widely made. Another is curaçao, originally a
triple-sec (implying a three-stage manufacturing

Napoleon brandy   77

process, rather than dryness). Triple-sec is actually sweeter than curaçao in most cases, and slightly less alcoholic. Cointreau, Grand Marnier, Van der Hum and numerous curaçaos belong to this family of orange-flavoured fruit liqueurs.

OTHER FRENCH LIQUEURS

The French imagination has assumed unbridled licence in the naming of some of its lesser known types of liqueur. 'Baiser d'Amour', for one, is an unspecified herbal 'kiss of love'. 'Donjon' seems to imply incarceration in a dungeon of almonds and cognac, the respective sources of its vaunted virility and digestibility. 'Cedratine' is made from a variety of Corsican lemon. 'Arquebuse', though named after a medieval portable gun, is made from 33 plants, plus leaves and roots. And 'Prune Benoit Serres' is made from plums and said to add a sparkle to your regard!

OUZO

An anis- or liquorice-flavoured liqueur that tastes marvellous as you read a Laurence Durrell book on the beach at Mykonos, listening to a bazoukia tune from a nearby taverna. As a tall drink, with ice, it is an agreeable preliminary to a kebab and most refreshing on a hot day. Clear and innocent-looking in the bottle, with water added it becomes milky white and more potent than you might expect.

P/Q

PARFAIT AMOUR

In days of old one of the best ways to provide sales of liqueurs was to claim for them some influence on a person's love life. Parfait Amour (perfect love), a sort of ratafia, is one of many such, whose name signals its aim: Venus Oil, Harem's Delight, Cream of the Virgin, were others. Some of these recipes have survived puritanism and revolution with less lurid names. Parfait Amour, coloured purple for passion, combines citrus and violets for flavour, and seems to be particularly popular in the U.S.A.

PASHA

As a Moslem country, Turkey produces grapes for the table rather than the bottle, but there are Turkish wines, of which Buzbag is the best-known red variety. Liqueur production, however, is limited to this sweetened extract of coffee.

PASTIS

A word used in southern France for any semi-liquid mixture, and applied by association to this combination of anis extract with water. Almost all Mediterranean countries make anis or pastis-type liqueurs, the former by macerating, the latter by distilling, anis and liquorice. Most makers also make anisette as well, a strong sweet spirit, flavoured with anis. Pastis was the legal replacement for absinthe when it was made illegal. Henri-Louis Pernod was originally an absinthe maker. His successors brought out a Pernod anis after World War I, when wormwood was banned as an ingredient. Paul Ricard was another manufacturer who followed a slightly different formula. The two companies eventually merged, and now control over three-quarters of the French market, to which they also offer their new invention of alcohol-free pastis, called Blancard or Pacific. Mrs Peter Hallgarten, the wife of Britain's leading liqueur maker, likes cooking kebabs with Pernod.

KEBABS WITH PERNOD. Use 1½ lb of sirloin cut into 1½ in chunks, and marinate them in 2 tablespoons of Pernod, ⅓ cup olive oil, 1 chopped onion and 1 pinch crushed fennel seed for 2 hours. Thread the meat on skewers, alternating meat, sliced fennel, squares of bacon and small onions (or onion slices). Grill them, basting occasionally with the marinade, for ten minutes or so. Serve with rice.

PEAR LIQUEURS

Made from Williams pears, this is a liqueur that really has the aroma of the fruit in it. Eau-de-vie de poires or poire Williams smells and tastes deliciously like pears and comes mainly from Switzerland, Alsace, Austria and Germany.

The Williams pear bud is sometimes thrust into a bottle and allowed to develop in this private hothouse until it is ripe, and too large to be extracted. The pear in the bottle is then pricked to allow its juices to escape, and drowned in pear brandy. The Swiss make the best, I think. This liqueur is especially flavourful when poured over fresh pineapple – the tastes complement each other perfectly.

PEPPERMINT LIQUEURS

There are many brands of crème de menthe, or peppermint liqueur. Both green and white versions

are available, but to my mind there's no point to the white one. My far-ahead favourite is Pippermint Get, a deep green delight in a curvaceous bottle; not too sweet, not too sharp, perfect both as a refreshing, taste-soothing aperitif or after-dinner drink. Today it is owned by the Bénédictine company. Other good varieties, which are a bit more stridently minty, are Freezomint by Cusenier, and Bols Crème de Menthe.

PIMMS

A famed, ready-mixed cocktail that has been sold in England for about 100 years. Basically it is a Gin-Sling (2 oz dry gin in a Highball glass with a teaspoon of sugar, ice and soda), to which other flavours of herbs and liqueurs have been added. The barman will usually add his own touch, with a sprig of mint, one of borage, a slice of cucumber, and possibly a lemon or orange slice. There used to be several different kinds with bases of whisky, brandy, rum, rye whiskey or vodka. Today only the gin and vodka versions are sold.

PIÑA COLADA

A new liqueur, low in alcoholic strength, which is made from rum and pineapples, flavoured with coconut – also a cocktail (see below).

PIÑA COLADA. Mix 2 oz each rum, coconut milk and crushed pineapple and blend with ice.

PINEAU

They were certainly accident-prone in ancient times! Pineau des Charentes is another in a long line of drinks 'discovered' by chance. This time a cellarmaster poured must (grape juice) into a cask in which some remains of cognac still lay. Being in no hurry, it took him 'several years' to clean out this cask, whereupon he found that it had turned into a clear, sweet, fruity wine 'of exceptional quality'. Amazingly enough, this became Pineau, now made with fresh cognac

grape-must, to which cognac is added to make a
'liqueur' (really a fortified wine) of around 17%
alcohol. It is usually drunk cold as an aperitif, but can
be used with desserts – especially good with melon.

PISCO

A grape brandy made in Chile and Peru from muscat
grapes, and full of their fruity aroma. Pisco taken by
itself as a liqueur brandy is delicious. A Pisco Sour is one
of the world's best cocktails.

**PISCO SOUR. Mix one part pisco with two parts fresh lime
juice and sugar to taste.**

POIRE WILLIAMS

A white spirit made from pears, with an aroma and a
taste to titillate the most blasé taste buds. (See *pear
liqueurs*.)

POTEEN

This is the Irish name, meaning 'a little pot', for illegally
distilled whiskey. Its quality varied tremendously, but
at its best, according to Irish connoisseurs, it was a very
good whiskey. In the U.S.A. the same type of illicit
distilling produced 'moonshine'.

PRUNELLE

The French for sloe (q.v.), and their name for a type of
sloe gin, or liqueur de prunelles. Sloe is another name
for blackthorn, a kind of wild plum.

PUNCH

A mixed drink, either hot or cold, made from spirits
and flavoured with lemons or other fruit, spices
and sugar, and sometimes prepared with milk. Cold
punch is often wine-based with a fruit flavouring, and
can be strengthened with vodka or rum.

PUNSCH

A Swedish speciality, made from Indonesian arrack (q.v.) blended with brandy and wines and aged for half a year. It can be drunk cold or hot. Not for the lily-livered!

PUNT-E-MES

An Italian bitter vermouth (q.v.) based on wine with a dose of quinine – an almost violent contrast of bitter with sweet; popular in Italy where they appreciate bitters as aperitifs. Good very cold, or on the rocks.

QUETSCH

The German name for clear, white plum brandy (also spelt Zwetschgen- or Zwetschenwasser). Quality, of course, differs from place to place, but you are almost sure of a good eau-de-vie if you order a quetsch in any of the German-speaking Eastern European countries and, in France, in Alsace. It is also known as slivovitz (spelt in various ways). This type of brandy is often very smooth and fruity.

QUININE

(Chinchona in Spanish, china in Italian.) The bark of a South American tree is the source of this bitter ingredient of many liqueurs and vermouths. It was originally included because of its medicinal value. (See also **china** and **quinquina**.)

QUINQUINA

A French bitter wine-vermouth, containing mistelles or grape juices which have only partially fermented, and made, as its name suggests, with a generous portion of quinine. Most widely found in the south of France, the best known brands are Byrrh, Dubonnet and St Raphaël.

RAKI

See **arrack**.

RATAFIA

A 'glass of something' that was drunk when a legal agreement was signed or 'ratified'. The drink itself could be made in several ways as a cordial, with fruit or nuts as flavouring and, as such, was probably the first true liqueur. It is today made by infusion of similar ingredients in wine spirits, sweetened, and sometimes has a herbal flavour added. Parfait Amour and St Raphaël are contemporary examples of ratafias.

RICARD

A well-known brand of pastis, made by Pernod.

RICE WINE

In China rice is used to make a kind of wine similar in strength to sherry and chiefly medicinal in its usage. Much rice 'wine' is homemade, somewhat like beer, by fermenting a rice mash, slightly sweetened, and with an alcohol content of from 8% to about 17%. Mao-Tai, made famous when President Nixon and Premier Chou En-Lai toasted their new friendship pact

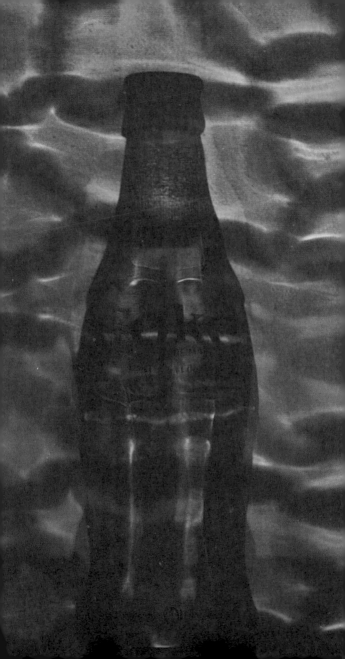

with it, is made from wheat and millet, has about 25%
alcohol, along with a peculiar and, to Westerners, not
very attractive taste.

*R*UM

Rum is a spirit distilled either from sugarcane juice, in
the old-fashioned way, or from molasses.

*R*um is made wherever sugar is grown – even in the
U.S.S.R. – but the Caribbean is its true home, where
some of it is as smooth as a fine liqueur brandy. In the
islands most people drink it almost as soon as it comes
out of the still. It is probably preferable, however, to
wait for a blender, a sort of spiritous adviser, to marry
the various types and give you a legitimately wedded
and properly matured blend. This takes about three
years, but rum continues to improve in oak casks for
twenty years or more.

*T*he French island of Martinique produces one of the
best rums, Rhum St James, made directly from
sugarcane juice in an amber and a white version, both
excellent. Haiti produces another cane juice rum,
Barbancourt, a marvellous, dark sipping rum, like
aged cognac. Cuba used to be the home of light
Bacardi until Castro took over. It is now made in Puerto
Rico (also known for Ron Rico) and several other
countries. The best-known brands from the island of
Jamaica are Appleton and Myers.

*R*um's flavour depends on the esters left in it. There are
almost as many flavours as there are islands in the
Caribbean. Rums tend to be darker and heavier the
farther south you get. Jamaican and Martiniquais
rums are the most highly flavoured. Some Jamaican
rum is like a black syrup, while Barilla rum from Puerto
Rico is almost as clear as gin. Guyanan Demerara
sometimes has ingredients like plums, raisins and
spice added to punches to give it a fruity taste. Pale
Gold Cuban rum is made from molasses. Barbados
rums are often flavoured with bitter almonds, sherry
and even raw steak.

*M*ost rum drinks are sweet because sugar or sweet

Rum mixer 87

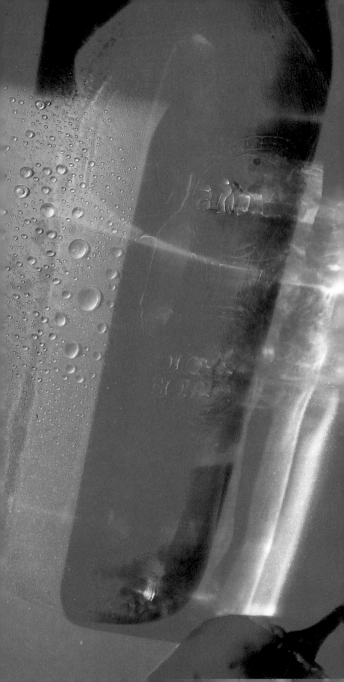

liqueur is often part of their recipe, but you can experiment with leaving out most or all of the sugar.

RUM PUNCH. *The Trinidadian version is made by mixing 1 bottle of dark rum with syrup (made with 1½ lb cane sugar in 1 quart of water, boiled until the sugar dissolves), the juice of 8 limes, and several dashes of Angostura bitters. Stir well and serve with crushed ice and a cherry. Sprinkle each drink with ginger or nutmeg. The longer it is kept, the better it becomes, so make a lot and keep it cold.*

PUNCH-À-CRÈME. *This needs 6 egg yolks beaten into 2 tins of evaporated milk and 1 tin condensed milk (depending on how rich and sweet you like it) until the mixture is thick and creamy. Into this pour ½ bottle dark rum, add several dashes Angostura and sprinkle the drinks with nutmeg.*

HOT BUTTERED. *Use 3 fl oz Jamaican rum, 3 cloves, 1 teaspoon brown sugar, pinch of cinnamon, 1 teaspoon unsalted butter. Dissolve the sugar in a tall glass in a drop of hot water and add the rest of the ingredients. Stand a spoon in the glass and fill with hot water.*

RUSSIAN FLAVOURED SPIRITS

The Russians, as a body, have a sweet tooth. Their wines are inclined to be syrupy, but their vodkas (q.v.) are mainly as dry as dry. There are many flavoured vodkas made by steeping various herbs in them. Some are very dry; some are sweetened with sugar. Starka (or brandy), the colour of strong tea, is aged in oak. Jarzebiak is flavoured with rowan berries. Pertsovka is reddish, flavoured with red peppers. Yubileynaya contains honey. Okhoichya contains eleven ingredients, including sugar. There are also quite admirable brandies from grape wine. Russians enjoy making liqueurs at home; one is a cherry spirit made by infusing sugared, fermented cherries in vodka. Wana Tallinn is a true liqueur, with orange and spice flavours, slightly bitter, and dark brown in colour.

RYE WHISKEY

An American type of whiskey made from rye instead of wheat. Rye was the main cereal available in colonial days, especially in Kentucky, though it is corn (maize) that goes into bourbon. Today rye takes second place to bourbon in American production.

SABRA

Israel's contribution to liqueurs, made with bitter Jaffa oranges and chocolate – a flavour combination which is rather sweet on the sip.

ST RAPHAËL

An example of ratafia (q.v.).

SAKE

Japanese rice wine, similar to the Chinese variety. It is not very alcoholic – about 17% – a bit like rather poor sherry. Traditionally, sake is served in small ceramic cups throughout a Japanese meal. It is usually drunk warm but can be served cold with ice. Sake is more a beer than a wine and has a bland taste. It is first brewed, then distilled.

SAMBUCA

A favourite Italian liqueur flavoured with liquorice and elderberry. Hence the name: Sambucus nigra is the botanical name for the elder tree. Tradition decrees it should be served with three (and only three) coffee beans floating on top, then set alight. A spectacular drink for the tête-a-tête!

SCHINKENHÄGER

This excellent German gin is a kind of schnapps made with juniper. It is usually drunk straight.

SCHNAPPS

An ancient Nordic-Germanic word used in Scandinavian and German-speaking countries. (Spelt schnaps in Denmark, snaps in Sweden and Norway.) Schnapps covers a multitude of spirits. It can be and is used in northern and eastern European countries for almost any kind of strong spirit, including whisky. Aquavit, German gins and what the French call eaux-de-vie are the most usual drinks referred to in this way. Dutch schnapps often have colourful names, like Venus Oil, Naked Navel or Lift your Shirt. Schnapps is usually drunk as an appetizer, with a beer 'chaser'. The St Bernard rescue dogs in the Swiss alps, in former days, actually carried schnapps, not brandy, in their little neck kegs. The Swiss also use it in emergencies for massaging torn muscles, and as an antiseptic.

SCOTCH WHISKY

Malt whisky is often treated like a liqueur, and deservedly so. (See **whisky**.)

SECRET

The most important word in the lexicon of the liqueur-manufacturing industry. Almost all liqueurs, vermouths or cordials claim they are made from a secret formula, usually discovered among the papers of a long-forgotten forebear by the present makers, or their predecessors! The secret usually involves the number and type of herbs or other flavourings used.

SLIVOVITZ

(The word is spelt slightly differently in parts of Eastern Europe.) A clear drink made from a mash of plums and

their crushed kernels, fermented and double-distilled. Yugoslavia is the prime source of slivovitz, but Bulgaria, Hungary, Germany and other countries also make it. Aged in wood for three to five years, it can be an excellent spirit, both aromatic and smooth.

SLOE GIN

Not necessarily a gin, but a neutral spirit to which sugar, but no juniper, is added, and in which the berries of sloe (which is a wild type of plum also called blackthorn) are steeped until the spirit takes on their flavour and colour. In France it is called Prunelle, where it is popular as a liqueur, and is a speciality of Burgundy. This is one of the easiest liqueurs to make at home. In England, at least, sloe berries grow wild in many parts of the country. Prick a pound of sloes thoroughly with a fork and place in a wide-mouthed bottle with 10 ounces of sugar. Fill the bottle with vodka or gin; seal the bottle and leave it for about three months, turning and shaking occasionally. Drain the lovely red-coloured spirit off and bottle it. A couple of weeks more of standing will do it no harm.

SOFT FRUIT LIQUEURS

Liqueurs made from raspberries, strawberries, cherries, peaches, plums or apricots. (see under individual names.)

SOUTHERN COMFORT

America's best-known liqueur, with its own secret formula that we suspect is an American whiskey with a flavouring of peaches from Georgia and oranges. Whatever it is, it makes a delectable drink. A soufflé made with Southern Comfort is a treat. Just add a jigger of the liqueur to your recipe for a four-person soufflé, and add some grated orange peel.

WHISKEY SOUR. 2 fl oz of Southern Comfort, 1 fl oz lemon juice and sugar to taste. Shake with cracked ice.

STEINHÄGER

Another good German gin with a powerful juniper flavour.

STOCK

A 100-year-old Italian firm that claims to be the biggest brandy-maker in the world, and also produces grappa, cherry brandy, Sambuca, Amaretto and other flavours of liqueurs.

STOLICHNAYA

A quality brand of Russian vodka, soft and flavourful, with an alcoholic content of 40%. It seems to demand blinis and caviare.

STREGA

An Italian liqueur, tasting a bit like Chartreuse, which is made from over 70 different herbs. They say Strega is magical – witches, disguised as beautiful maidens, are supposed to have blended it to a formula that ensures any couples who taste it together will be forever united – fine for lovers, but possibly confusing if the couple are enemies.

*T*EA LIQUEURS

Something of an oddity, tea-liqueurs are mainly made in Japan, though it may still be possible to find an occasional European tea-liqueur, like Marie Brizard's Tea Breeze. A very sweet Japanese version is Ocha Green Tea by Suntory, combining brandy and tea in a pottery bottle. Matcha and Gyokuro are other tea-liqueur names, also extremely sweet. Possibly best as a sweetener in place of sugar in iced tea.

*T*EQUILA

Tequila is distilled from the sour juice of the fully matured heart of the century plant, or agave. It comes in a water-white and a golden version, both aged in oak. It tastes sharper and tarter than gin or vodka. It takes eight to twelve years for an agave plant to be ready to harvest. Each pineapple-shaped heart is about 45cm (18in) in diameter and 60cm (2ft) tall, and needs to be chopped from its protective surrounding of prickly, sword-like leaves. From the juice a sort of beer, called pulque, is made. This is distilled into a rough liquor called mezcal, which is redistilled into tequila. In effect tequila is an appellation contrôlée beverage since only this second distillation from the towns of Tequila, Arenal, Amatitla, Arandas and the region around Guadalajara is allowed to use the name.

> **MARGARITA.** This is the best-known tequila-based cocktail. For a Margarita punch put ½ pint lime juice with ½ pint Cointreau (or triple-sec) in a blender for two or three seconds. Dip the rims of Old-Fashioned glasses into the liquid, then into a thin sprinkling of salt. To the juice and Cointreau, add 1 pint of tequila, and the whites of two eggs, then fill the blender with crushed ice and run it until the ice is mushy. Fill the salt-encrusted glasses with this mix. This should serve about 18 to 20 people. About two glasses per person is about all you can handle at a sitting!

TIA MARIA

A liqueur made in Jamaica with fine five-year-old Jamaican rum, and the best coffee in the world, Blue Mountain. Not overly sweet, which may account for its being one of the top selling after-dinner liqueurs.

> **OJ-MARIA.** This calls for a tall glass filled with cracked ice. Over this pour 1½ fl oz Tia Maria and fill up with fresh orange juice. Wonderfully refreshing.

TORRES

Gran Torres Liquor is a Spanish blend of pot-still brandy with extracts of macerated orange, aromatic herbs, sugar and honey, aged in American oak.

TRAPPISTINE

A French liqueur made by Trappist monks of the Abbey de la Grace de Dieu. It is based on armagnac and local herbs from the mountains around Doubs, on the Swiss frontier.

TRIPLE-SEC

A generic term used widely in Spain (the Spanish equivalent is triple seco), France and South America for a clear, orange-flavoured liqueur which, despite its name – meaning triple-dry – is very sweet. Cointreau originally called itself Triple-sec, but changed to its present name because of imitations. Curaçao was also called Triple-sec when it was first launched, and a white version is still made, called Curaçao Triple-sec.

/U/V/W/

U ISGE BAUGH

Celtic for 'water of life', and spelt in various ways; usge beatha is one example. It is supposed to be the basis for the word whisky or whiskey.

U NDERBERG

A medicinal German bitters, something like Fernet Branca (q.v.), and very effective as a hangover cure. It is also recommended by its makers as either an aperitif or a digestif. It combines German brandy with herbs, which give it its main aroma, and bark and root flavours. Sold in small, one-drink bottles.

U NICUM

Another famed bitters, this time made in Italy and in Austria by Zwack, where liqueurs have been preferred to most other spirits ever since the Austro-Hungarian Empire and the heyday of the coffee house. Unicum is slightly sweeter than Angostura or Underberg, but used in the same ways.

U SHER

In about 1853 a citizen of Edinburgh named Andrew Usher discovered that non-Scots liked their malt blended with grain whisky, and began to export this new blend. Sales boomed, but the Scots complained the blend was not 'whisky', and brought a suit – the famous 'What is Whisky?' case. In 1909 a Royal commission finally determined that even continuously distilled grain whisky could be called 'Scotch' as long as it was made in Scotland. Most of the Scotch we drink today is blended – the best thing that ever happened to the Scotch industry.

VAN DER HUM

Made in South Africa from Cape brandy, in which naartjies, a South African type of tangerine, are macerated, spiced with nutmeg and other herbs, and laced with spirits. Pale yellow in colour, it is completely drinkable, fresh-tasting, and a good digestif.

VANILLE, Crème de

Alexandre Dumas said that vanilla is 'an exotic plant whose aroma is so agreeable it is used to flavour liqueurs'. You can make your own vanilla ratafia by infusing three vanilla pods in a bottle of vodka for a couple of weeks, then blending the infusion with thick sugar syrup. Filter, bottle and sip!

VERMOUTH

Not quite a spirit, nor a liqueur, but a beverage made by adding flavours to wine that bridges the gap between the two. Italy is the largest producer, France the runner-up. In a way, it is a milder form of bitters, usually containing a portion of that ubiquitous, acrid, medicinal ingredient, quinine. Vermouth has always been made with 40 or 50 'secret' ingredients, which include many herbs chosen both for their aromatic and medicinal properties.
In France the herbs for vermouth are usually macerated directly in fortified wines. In Italy they normally give up their flavours and aromas by

percolation, through wines high in alcohol content, or through spirits. In France and Italy, the countries that have set the standards for vermouths, they are often drunk as aperitifs with ice and soda; so too in South America. In the rest of the Western World, however, they are mainly regarded as mixers, and used to add flavour to other drinks, in cocktails.

There are two principal types, white and red. The white is normally the drier of the two, the red more pungent and sweet. Alcoholic strength is around 16%. Both French and Italian makers produce dry as well as sweet vermouths. Italian producers include Martini & Rossi, Cinzano, and others. The biggest French producer is Noilly Prat.

In Chile, the aperitif-vermouth-hour is such a tradition that the first cinema show of the evening, at cocktail time, is called 'the vermouth show'. Vermouth is derived from the German, wermut, which means wormwood, originally an ingredient of early types.

HOT STUFF. Mix 1 fl oz Campari with 1 fl oz dry white vermouth (or to taste). Shake with ice.
MACA. Mix 1 fl oz each red and white martini vermouth with ¼ fl oz of cassis. Shake with ice.
DRY MARTINI. Mix five to ten parts gin and one part dry white vermouth. Stir or shake and serve with lemon peel.

VERVEINE DU VELAY

This Auvergnat liqueur from France, one of my favourites, has a nicely bitter tang to it that comes from its main flavouring ingredient, verbena, and 32 other herbs. Two versions are available, the yellow and a stronger green one based on brandy, to which honey is added.

VIEILLE CURE

Originally a monastic 'cure', or medicine, this was a blend of some 50 herbs with brandy, produced at the Abbaye de Cenon, near Bordeaux. Now made by Intermarque, the same firm that makes Cordial Médoc. Fairly dry as liqueurs go.

VILLANOVA, Arnaldo de

A thirteenth-century Spanish Catalan doctor who lived in France where he was known as Arnaud de Villeneuve. He was physician to kings and the French popes who resided at Avignon. It is said that he was the first to make liqueurs by distilling wine with herbs and spices. (However, the Romans flavoured their wines, as, possibly, did the Arabs, who, with their knowledge of distillation, may have experimented with flavoured alcohols much earlier.) By saving the life of one Pope, Arnaldo de Villanova saved himself from the tortures of the Spanish Inquisition, it is said.

VIOLETTES, Crème de

A very sweet liqueur, the flavour of which is derived from violet petals. The only one I know of was made in the U.S.A. and named for Yvette Gilbert, dancer and model for Toulouse Lautrec. A liqueur infusion of violet petals was considered useful as a reviver of geriatrics in Dumas' day!

VODKA

Vodka has no taste in its pristine form, and no smell, so it will mix with anything. In Iran, for instance, where some of the best vodka used to be made, they had a deliciously refreshing summer drink called abdug made from vodka and yogurt. Put equal quantities of soda water and plain yogurt in a tumbler, add a sprig of spearmint, if you fancy the taste, and a measure of vodka topped off with a pinch of salt.

Vodka is best served spectacularly encased in ice. Put the spirit into a small carafe. Place the carafe in a tin large enough to hold it plus enough water to surround the carafe. Put all this into the freezer. When the water is frozen, dip the tin in hot water for a moment, slide the iced tin off, and what you get at the table is a handsome block of ice surrounding the vodka. Just the right temperature for imbibing. This icy treat is most often drunk with caviar.

*T*he Russians and Poles drink with such light-hearted speed because they are afraid of becoming drunk on the fumes. They claim that by sipping you inhale more alcohol than you drink. They like it, as they say, with a tear – that is, with the outside of the glass frosted with cold. And they like it coloured and flavoured by the addition of various herbs. Saffron makes it yellow, sunflower seeds give a mauve tint, cornflowers turn it blue and walnut shells brown.

*A*s to taste, you can vary that too, whether with rowan berry, cherry, honey or red pepper. Russian vodka used to be made from potatoes. Now most of it is made from grain, but it can all be flavoured. My favourite is the Polish version of Zubrovka (the Russians make this too), which contains a slip of the herb of that name, a grass on which the European bison feeds. This herb gives the vodka a pleasant nutty taste and a slightly green tinge.

*I*f you start with vodka, switch to wine during a meal, and go back to vodka – you can still hold your head high the next morning. Possibly this is because vodka is very 'pure'. It is distilled twice, then filtered through charcoal to rid it of all taste or smell. According to hospital research on hangovers, a mixture of pure alcochol and orange juice is the most 'clear-headed' alcoholic thing to drink. Anyone can make this famous drink – a Screwdriver – which was supposedly invented by American oil rig workmen who stirred their concoction with the eponymous instrument.

COFFEE VODKA. You will need 4 cups of sugar, water and vodka and ½ lb freshly ground coffee. Pour 1 cup of vodka over the raw grounds and let it sit for a week. Make sugar and water into syrup and add it to the rest of the vodka. Then combine coffee vodka with syrup vodka, strain, bottle and store for six months to let it all blend smoothly. Depending on your intestinal fortitude, you can then drink or sip.

LEMON VODKA. Grate the rind of 3 lemons (or use 2 oranges instead), cover it with vodka and allow to stand for four days or so. Make a syrup of 2 cups each of water and sugar. Strain the rind out of the vodka and pour both the lemony vodka and the rest of the bottle (about 4 cups) into the syrup while it is still hot. Strain the whole thing again, bottle and store for at least a month.

TARRAGON VODKA. This is easy – put some fresh tarragon into the bottle and let it sit for a week or two.

WHITE SHOULDERS. *Take a measure of vodka, half a measure of curaçao, and one of heavy cream. Mix in a blender, and serve in a large glass over ice.*
BLACK COSSACK. *Put a measure of vodka in a tall glass, then fill with cold Guinness.*
RASPUTIN. *Put a measure of vodka in a tall glass with ice, fill with clam juice, and add an anchovy-stuffed olive.*
VODKA BLOODSHOT. *Mix equal parts vodka, tomato juice and canned consommé with the juice of half a lemon and a dash of Worcestershire sauce.*
GREEN TREETOP. *Mix equal parts vodka and lemon juice with a little sugar to taste. Pour over ice and serve with chopped mint and a drop of crème de menthe.*

WASSER

The German word for water, which, when applied to liqueurs, means any clear, water-white spirit distilled from fermented fruit, fruit juices or fruit kernels without any sweetening. The word is added, as is the German usage, to the name of the fruit involved – Kirschwasser is cherry spirit, Zwetschgenwasser is plum spirit, and so on.

WHISKY

Today's multi-million-dollar whisky industry began its career hidden away in gullies, bothies, byres, craggy mountain-sides and dark caverns. Pioneer, in whisky terms, generally meant smuggler. Even King George IV (according to a whisky historian, A. Barnard, writing in 1887) liked Highland malt whisky, then the drink among connoisseurs, and would drink nothing but pure, illegal Glenlivet. The list of former bootleg stills is long and contains names that are among the most distinguished of modern brands – Glenlivet, Cardhu (which goes into Johnny Walker), Macallan and many of the Islay whiskies.

Because so much of its early manufacture had to be done in a great hurry to evade the law, some old stills could convert 80 gallons of mash into whisky in three and a half minutes, so Barnard tells us. This whisky was naturally rather rough, but such experiments did eventually cause serious technicians to investigate the quality-speed balance.

In 1830, Aeneas Coffey, a former Inspector-General of Excise for Ireland, perfected a continuous way of distilling that could produce up to 1,000 gallons of alcohol an hour. The oceans of whisky that poured from Mr Coffey's stills were made from grain and were neutral in taste – quite different from the original Scotch, made from malted barley in pot-stills. It could be turned into industrial alcohol or gin as easily as it could be turned into whisky.

The new form of alcohol was used for blending with malt whisky to reduce its strong, peaty, smoky flavour, which seemed too powerful for any but a true Scot to drink in any quantity. Enough malt flavour remained in this blend to satisfy the customers, and it had the added advantage of allowing the final product to be sold at far lower prices than the pure malts.

Modern distilling has brought many changes since the days of the bootlegger. One main difference is in hygiene – today's Scotch distilleries maintain a state of cleanliness that is, as nearly as possible, sterile. Another is the emphasis on conservation – reusing waste products for heating, for instance.

Quality in malt whisky, the Scotch experts say, depends on three things. First, the shape of the pot-still that maintains the best possible flavour and aroma in the distilling process. Second, the quality of water used to reduce the alcoholic strength to drinkable levels (70% in Britain). It must be pure and devoid of minerals – in fact demineralized water is now used in most distilleries, rather than the old-time 'pure burn water'. Third, the way the malt is 'peated'.

Malt is barley that has been caused to sprout by dampening it. It is then roasted over peat fires whose 'reek' (smoke) filters through the sprouted grain and gives it the tarred rope taste beloved of malt fans.

Malt is the liqueur of the whisky world, and an absolutely essential element in its blending. It is a mysterious spirit. On Speyside, quite dissimilar single malts are produced in distilleries at almost identical locations, with similar ingredients and equipment.

The Glenfiddich and Balvenie buildings are across the road from each other. They use the same water supply, peat and distilling procedures. The only apparent distinction is in the shapes of their respective still-heads. Nevertheless the two establishments produce quite different results – both, fortunately, extremely agreeable to drink.

*T*he saying is that any good Scotch blend must contain, among its 30 or 40 different types of whisky, a Highland malt, a Lowland malt, an island malt and a grain whisky. The island that makes the most pungent of malts is Islay, about an hour's air-trip from Glasgow. Islay was once a smuggler's paradise. Now it is a quiet resort, with huge reserves of peat and several distilleries making its name famous.

*M*ost Scottish distilleries are in pretty surroundings. If ever you get a chance to visit them, do. You will be sure to have a warm welcome, and possibly a sample of their work. (See also **American whiskey, bourbon whiskey, Canadian whisky, Irish whiskey, malt whisky, rye whiskey**.)

*W*HITE SPIRITS

These are what the French call *alcool blanc* and the Germans call schnapps (q.v.). They are usually pure distillations of fruit, from pears, cherries and plums, to raspberries and strawberries. They are very fragrant and usually have a definite taste of the fruit they are made from. They can also be water-white liqueurs like kümmel or quetsch (q.v.). You drink them straight, in small glasses.

*W*ILLIAMS

A deliciously aromatic liqueur, made in many countries. The best are from Switzerland, Alsace, Germany and Australia. You may have tried pineapple with kirsch, but you have never really tasted pineapple unless you have had it with Williams. (See also **poire Williams**.)

XYZ

XANTHIA

A liqueur cocktail made with yellow Chartreuse, cherry brandy and gin, in equal quantities. It is shaken with ice before serving.

XENOPHON

Even in the day of the Greek historian and Athenian general (c.430–c.356 B.C.), rich Persian connoisseurs were ardent collectors of 'drinking vessels' (which I interpret with some literary licence as liqueur glasses).

XERES

The only alcoholic beverage that comes anywhere near being spelt with an X is this one. Xeres is the French name for what the Spaniards would put under J (jerez), and the Anglo-Saxons under S (sherry), which is, in a way, a liqueur wine, like port, according to my favourite source of dubious knowledge, Alexandre Dumas. In his Grand Dictionnaire de Cuisine, Dumas' entry for Xeres reads: '. . . We've already spoken enough about this in our article on foreign wines.' That article states that Xeres is the second best of Spanish white wines, without other comment. Xeres may also be a cocktail of 2 fl oz sherry with a dash each of peach and orange bitters stirred with ice.

XOCHIMILCOS

Coffee liqueur and cream – 2 fl oz Kahlúa with ½ fl oz cream floating on top.

YQUEM, Château d'

This Sauternes grand premier cru is one of the great wines of the world. Tops in after-dinner wines, and almost a liqueur, Yquem lives longer than most wines. H. Warner Allen, the late, great expert and journalist, drank a Château d'Yquem that was 80 years old, but still full of 'teeth and fire and generosity', he claimed.

YUGOSLAVIA

The original home of slivovitz, where the Dalmatian coast provides the plums that make this a brandy of great quality, dry white, with a delicate bouquet, and strong withal. Dalmatia also grows the little black cherries that are turned into Maraschino, one of the best-known cherry brandies.

ZUBROVKA

A flavoured vodka, made both in Poland and the U.S.S.R., both of which claim to be the first to have made it. Personally, I prefer the Polish version, but both are excellent, with a subtle herby taste imparted by steeping a blade of buffalo grass in the spirit.

ZWACK

A 150-year-old Viennese firm which even at its inception had some 220 liqueurs on its list of products. Some, including Viennese Pear, Apricot and Café, are still in their modern catalogue. They claim that the pear is the only fruit that ripens from the core out. So they only use the inner flesh for their liqueur. The apricot, on the other hand, is distilled whole, and their coffee beans are the aristocrats of the coffee world. (See also **unicum**.)

*I*NDEX